LIFE SKILLS FOR TEENAGE BOYS

PRACTICAL ADVICE FOR PERSONAL GROWTH,
BECOMING INDEPENDENT, AND TRANSITIONING TO
ADULTHOOD WITH 100+ PROVEN STRATEGIES.

A.E NICHOLLS

Akeso
PUBLISHING

DEDICATION

To all the incredible teenage boys out there navigating the rollercoaster ride of adolescence, this book is for you. As an occupational therapist, I've witnessed firsthand the triumphs and struggles you face every day. Your stories, your resilience, and your unbreakable spirit have not only inspired the words on these pages but have also taught me more about life than I ever could have imagined.

To my amazing clients, who bravely share their journeys with me---you are the heart and soul of this book. Your experiences have shaped every chapter, every piece of advice, and every moment of laughter and tears. Thank you for trusting me to be a part of your lives and for showing me the true meaning of strength and perseverance.

May this book be a guiding light, a source of enjoyment, and a reminder that you are not alone on this wild journey of teenage life. Here's to embracing the chaos, celebrating the victories, and discovering the incredible potential within each and every one of you.

With love and admiration,

A.E. Nicholls

CONTENTS

INTRODUCTION

"Making your mark on the world is hard. If it were easy, everybody would do it. But it's not. It takes patience, it takes commitment, and it comes with plenty of failure along the way. The real test is not whether you avoid this failure, because you won't. It's whether you let it harden or shame you into inaction, or whether you learn from it; whether you choose to persevere" - Barack Obama.

Welcome to "Life Skills for Teenage Boys," a comprehensive guide designed to help you navigate the exciting and sometimes challenging journey of adolescence. As you stand on the brink of adulthood, you'll face many new experiences, responsibilities, and decisions that will shape your future. You're at a crossroads, teenage guys. The path ahead is filled with choices that'll shape who you become. It's more than just that group project due next week or studying for the big test. It's about navigating the ups and downs of growing up, figuring out who you are, and learning how to take on the real world.

That's where this book comes in. I'm an occupational therapist who's spent years working with teenagers just like you. I've heard your stories, your struggles, and your dreams. And I'm here to guide you on this wild ride called adolescence.

"Life Skills for Teenage Boys" is all about giving you the tools to crush it in life. We're talking practical, down-to-earth advice that explains 'why', giving you the meaning and reasoning you need. This book is like your personal coach, breaking it all down in a language you'll actually understand.

Developing life skills early on can have significant long-term benefits for your personal, academic, and professional success. By learning how to take care of yourself, manage your emotions, build strong relationships, and make informed decisions about your future, you'll be well-equipped to handle the challenges and opportunities that come with adulthood.

In the following chapters, we'll explore a wide range of topics, from self-care and mental health to financial literacy, career planning, and cultural competence. Each section is packed with practical advice, real-life examples, expert insights, and actionable strategies to help you develop the skills and confidence to succeed in all areas of your life. And you'll learn it in a way that feels natural, not like you're being lectured by some out-of-touch adult.

Here's the deal: growing up is tough, but you've got this. You're stronger than you think, and this book is your backup, your support system, your secret weapon. It's time to take control of your life and start adulting like a pro.

So, what are you waiting for? Whether you're just starting high school or preparing for college and beyond, this book will be your companion and guide, offering support, encouragement, and the tools you need to make the most of your teenage years. So, let's dive in and start building the foundation for a bright, successful future.

EMOTIONAL INTELLIGENCE AND SELF-AWARENESS

"Self-awareness — recognizing a feeling as it happens — is the keystone of emotional intelligence." - Daniel Goleman.

Emotional intelligence (EI) is the ability to understand and manage your own emotions, as well as recognize and influence the emotions of others. Self-awareness, or the ability to accurately perceive your own emotions, thoughts, and values, is a key component of emotional intelligence. Developing these skills can help you build stronger relationships, make better decisions, and navigate the challenges of adolescence with greater resilience and adaptability.

Developing emotional intelligence and self-awareness is crucial for teenage boys because:

- It helps you better understand and regulate your own emotions, leading to improved mental health and well-being.
- It enables you to build and maintain strong, healthy relationships with family, friends, and romantic partners.
- It improves your ability to communicate effectively, resolve conflicts, and collaborate with others.

- It enhances your decision-making skills and helps you align your actions with your values and goals.
- It increases your resilience and adaptability in the face of challenges and setbacks.
- It sets you up for success in future academic, career, and personal endeavors.

THE FOUR COMPONENTS OF EMOTIONAL INTELLIGENCE

According to psychologist Daniel Goleman (2018), there are four main components of emotional intelligence:

Self-awareness: The ability to recognize and understand your own emotions, strengths, weaknesses, and values.

Self-management: The ability to regulate and control your emotions and impulses and adapt to changing circumstances.

Social awareness: The ability to understand and empathize with others' emotions and perspectives.

Relationship management: The ability to communicate effectively, resolve conflicts, and build positive relationships with others.

EXPERT INSIGHT: THE IMPORTANCE OF EMOTIONAL INTELLIGENCE

Dr. Sarah Johnson, a psychologist, explains the significance of emotional intelligence for teenage boys:

"Emotional intelligence is a crucial skill for success in all areas of life, from personal relationships to academic and career achievement. Research has shown that people with high emotional intelligence tend to have better mental health, more satisfying relationships, and greater leadership potential.

As a teenager, developing your emotional intelligence can help you navigate the challenges of adolescence with greater resilience and adaptability. It can also set you up for long-term success by giving you the tools to communicate effectively, manage stress, and build strong, supportive relationships."

STRATEGIES FOR DEVELOPING SELF-AWARENESS

Developing self-awareness is an ongoing process that requires intro-spection, honesty, and a willingness to learn and grow. Here's why each strategy is important:

Practice mindfulness: Mindfulness helps you stay present and attuned to your inner experiences, increasing your ability to recognize and understand your emotions, thoughts, and behaviors in the moment.

Keep a journal: Journaling allows you to process and reflect on your experiences, emotions, and patterns over time, providing valuable insights into your inner world and growth areas.

Seek feedback: Receiving honest feedback from others can help you gain a more accurate and well-rounded understanding of your strengths, weaknesses, and blind spots, which may be difficult to see on your own.

Take personality assessments: Personality assessments can provide a framework for understanding your unique traits, preferences, and tendencies, helping you better understand yourself and how you relate to others.

Reflect on your values: Clarifying your values helps you develop a strong sense of identity and purpose, guiding your decisions and actions in a way that aligns with your authentic self.

INTERACTIVE ACTIVITY: MINDFULNESS MEDITATION

Try this simple mindfulness meditation to practice self-awareness:

1. Find a quiet, comfortable place to sit or lie down.

2. Close your eyes and take a few deep breaths, focusing on the sensation of the breath moving in and out of your body.

3. Notice any thoughts, feelings, or physical sensations that arise without trying to change or judge them.

4. If your mind starts to wander, gently redirect your attention back to your breath.

5. Continue for 5-10 minutes, or longer if desired.

Regular mindfulness practice can help you develop greater self-awareness, reduce stress and anxiety, and improve focus and concentration.

MANAGING EMOTIONS EFFECTIVELY

In addition to recognizing your emotions, it's important to learn how to manage them effectively. Here's why each strategy is valuable:

Practice self-care: Engaging in self-care activities helps reduce stress, improve mood, and increase overall well-being, making it easier to regulate your emotions and respond to challenges in a healthy way.

Use positive self-talk: Positive self-talk helps counteract negative thought patterns, builds self-confidence, and increases motivation, enabling you to approach difficult situations with a more optimistic and resilient mindset.

Develop a support system: Having a strong support system provides a safe space to express your emotions, receive encouragement and advice, and feel validated and understood, which is essential for emotional well-being.

Practice assertive communication: Assertive communication helps you express your needs, thoughts, and feelings in a clear, respectful manner, reducing misunderstandings and conflicts, and fostering healthier relationships.

Use healthy coping mechanisms:

Employing healthy coping strategies helps you process and manage difficult emotions in a constructive way, preventing the buildup of stress and negative feelings that can lead to poor decision-making or unhealthy behaviors.

REAL-LIFE STORY: HOW EMOTIONAL INTELLIGENCE HELPED ME OVERCOME BULLYING

David, a high school junior, shares how developing emotional intelligence skills helped him navigate a difficult experience with bullying:

"When I was in middle school, I was bullied by a group of boys who made fun of my appearance and interests. I felt hurt, angry, and alone. I didn't know how to cope with my emotions or stand up for myself.

That's when I started learning about emotional intelligence. I realized that I needed to develop greater self-awareness and self-management skills to handle the bullying effectively. I started keeping a journal to track my emotions and practice positive self-talk. I also reached out to my school counselor and joined a support group for students who had experienced bullying.

As I developed my emotional intelligence, I became better at regulating my emotions and communicating my needs assertively. I learned how to set boundaries with the bullies and surround myself with positive, supportive friends.

Now, I use my emotional intelligence skills to navigate the challenges of teenage life. I'm better able to manage stress, build strong relationships, and make decisions that align with my values and goals. I know that these skills will serve me well throughout my life."

KEY TAKEAWAYS

- Emotional intelligence involves understanding and managing your own emotions, as well as recognizing and influencing others' emotions.
- Developing self-awareness is key to building emotional intelligence and involves practices like mindfulness, journaling, and seeking feedback.
- Learning to manage emotions effectively involves self-care, positive self-talk, assertive communication, and healthy coping mechanisms.

- Emotional intelligence skills are crucial for navigating the challenges of adolescence and setting yourself up for long-term success in relationships, academics, and career.

2

MENTAL HEALTH AND WELLNESS

"Everyone is going through something that we can't see. The thing is, because we can't see it, we don't know who's going through what and how much they're struggling. The key thing is, regardless of how it may appear on the outside, you have to speak up and not bottle it up." (Kevin Love, 2018)

As a teenage boy, navigating the challenges of adolescence can be overwhelming at times. Between academic pressures, social dynamics, and the physical and emotional changes of puberty, it's common to experience stress, anxiety, and other mental health challenges. Prioritizing mental health and developing effective coping strategies is crucial for teenage boys because:

- It helps you better manage stress, anxiety, and other common challenges of adolescence.
- It supports your overall well-being, happiness, and life satisfaction.
- It improves your ability to form and maintain healthy relationships with others.

- It enhances your academic performance and future career success.
- It reduces the risk of developing more severe mental health issues later in life.
- It empowers you to face adversity with resilience and adaptability.

COMMON MENTAL HEALTH CHALLENGES FOR TEENAGE BOYS

Some of the most common mental health challenges faced by teenage boys include:

Depression: Persistent feelings of sadness, hopelessness, and loss of interest in activities, which can interfere with daily functioning and relationships (Mojtabai et al., 2016).

Anxiety: Excessive worry, fear, or nervousness about everyday situations, which can lead to physical symptoms like a racing heart, sweating, or trembling (Merikangas et al., 2010).

Substance abuse: Misuse of alcohol, drugs, or other substances as a way to cope with stress, emotional pain, or peer pressure, which can lead to addiction and other health problems (Johnston et al., 2021).

Eating disorders: Unhealthy attitudes and behaviors related to food, weight, and body image, such as restrictive dieting, binge eating, or excessive exercise (Sweeting et al., 2015).

Trauma and stress-related disorders: Emotional or psychological distress related to experiencing or witnessing a traumatic event, such as abuse, violence, or a serious accident (McLaughlin et al., 2013).

It's important to remember that experiencing mental health challenges is not a sign of weakness or personal failure. Mental health conditions are real, treatable illnesses that affect people of all backgrounds and identities. Seeking help and support is a sign of strength and self-care.

REAL-LIFE EXAMPLE: OVERCOMING DEPRESSION AND ANXIETY

Ethan, a 16-year-old high school student, shares his experience with depression and anxiety and how he learned to cope:

"From the outside, it probably looked like I had it all together - I was a straight-A student, a varsity athlete, and had a solid group of friends. But inside, I was struggling with overwhelming feelings of sadness, self-doubt, and worry.

It started with small things, like having trouble sleeping or losing interest in activities I used to enjoy. But over time, the feelings got worse and started to interfere with my daily life. I had trouble concentrating in class, I lost my appetite, and started isolating myself from friends and family.

At first, I was ashamed to admit that I was struggling. I thought that as a guy, I was supposed to be tough and handle everything on my own. But as the symptoms worsened, I realized I needed help.

I started by talking to my parents about what I was going through. It was a difficult conversation, but they were incredibly supportive and helped me connect with a therapist who specialized in working with teenagers.

Through therapy, I learned coping strategies for managing my depression and anxiety, such as deep breathing, challenging negative thoughts, and setting realistic goals for myself. I also started making lifestyle changes, like getting regular exercise, eating a balanced diet, and prioritizing sleep.

It wasn't an easy journey, and there were still days when I struggled. But with the support of my therapist, family, and friends, I slowly started to feel like myself again. I learned that taking care of my mental health was just as important as taking care of my physical health.

Now, as I navigate the ups and downs of teenage life, I know that I have the tools and support system to cope with challenges in a healthy way. I've also become more open about my experience with mental health in hopes of reducing the stigma and encouraging other guys to seek help if they need it.

Looking back, I'm grateful for the journey I've been on. While I wouldn't wish depression or anxiety on anyone, I believe that facing these challenges has made me a stronger, more resilient person. I've learned the importance of self-care, asking for help, and prioritizing my well-being - lessons that will serve me well throughout my life."

STRATEGIES FOR COPING WITH STRESS AND ANXIETY

While some level of stress and anxiety is a normal part of life, chronic or severe symptoms can take a toll on your mental and physical health. Here are some strategies for coping with stress and anxiety in a healthy way:

Practice relaxation techniques: Deep breathing, progressive muscle relaxation, mindfulness meditation, and yoga are all evidence-based techniques for reducing stress and promoting relaxation (Khoury et al., 2015).

Exercise regularly: Physical activity releases endorphins, improves mood, and reduces stress and anxiety. Aim for at least 30 minutes of moderate exercise most days of the week (Sharma et al., 2006).

Get enough sleep: Lack of sleep can exacerbate stress and anxiety. Aim for 8-10 hours of sleep per night, and practice good sleep hygiene, such as avoiding screens before bed and creating a relaxing bedtime routine (Baglioni et al., 2016).

Connect with others: Social support is a powerful buffer against stress and anxiety. Make time for activities with friends and family, and don't hesitate to reach out for help when needed (Ozbay et al., 2007).

Practice time management: Feeling overwhelmed by tasks and responsibilities can contribute to stress and anxiety. Use tools like calendars, to-do lists, and prioritization to manage your time effectively and reduce feelings of overwhelm (Misra & McKean, 2000).

Challenge negative thoughts: Stress and anxiety often involve negative or catastrophic thinking patterns. Practice identifying and challenging these thoughts and replacing them with more balanced, realistic perspectives (Hofmann et al, 2012).

INTERACTIVE ACTIVITY: STRESS MANAGEMENT TOOLBOX

To help you develop a personalized stress management plan, try creating a stress management toolbox. This is a collection of strategies, activities, and resources that you can turn to when feeling stressed or anxious.

Brainstorm a list of stress management techniques that you find helpful or would like to try, such as deep breathing exercises, progressive muscle relaxation, mindfulness meditation, yoga, journaling, listening to music or nature sounds, spending time in nature, or engaging in a hobby or creative activity.

For each technique, identify any resources or materials you might need, such as guided meditation scripts, yoga mats, journals, or art supplies.

Create a physical or digital "toolbox" to store your stress management resources. This could be a box, binder, or folder on your computer or phone.

Whenever you're feeling stressed or anxious, turn to your toolbox and choose a technique to practice. Experiment with different strategies to find what works best for you in different situations.

Regularly update and refresh your toolbox with new ideas and resources as you discover them.

By having a go-to set of stress management tools at your fingertips, you'll be better equipped to handle the inevitable challenges and stressors of teenage life in a healthy, proactive way.

WHEN TO SEEK PROFESSIONAL HELP

While self-care strategies can be effective for managing mild to moderate stress and anxiety, there may be times when professional help is needed. Here are some signs that it might be time to seek support from a mental health professional:

- Persistent or severe symptoms of depression, anxiety, or other mental health conditions that interfere with daily functioning.
- Thoughts of self-harm or suicide.
- Difficulty coping with a traumatic event or significant life stressor.
- Substance abuse or addiction.
- Significant changes in mood, behavior, or academic performance.

If you or someone you know is experiencing these or other concerning symptoms, don't hesitate to reach out for help. Talk to a trusted adult, such as a parent, teacher, or school counselor, who can connect you with appropriate resources and support.

You can also contact national hotlines or organizations for immediate support and referrals, such as:

- National Suicide Prevention Lifeline: 1-800-273-TALK (8255).
- Crisis Text Line: Text "HOME" to 741741.
- National Alliance on Mental Illness (NAMI) Helpline: 1-800-950-NAMI (6264).

Remember, seeking help for mental health challenges is a sign of strength, not weakness. By prioritizing your mental health and wellness, you're setting yourself up for success and resilience in all areas of your life.

EXPERT INSIGHT: THE POWER OF MENTAL HEALTH LITERACY

Dr. Stephen Hinshaw, a professor of psychology at the University of California, Berkeley, and author of "Another Kind of Madness: A Journey Through the Stigma and Hope of Mental Illness," emphasizes the importance of mental health literacy for teenage boys:

"Mental health literacy - the knowledge and beliefs about mental disorders that aid in their recognition, management, or prevention - is a crucial skill for teenage boys to develop. By learning about the signs and symptoms of common mental health conditions, the available treatments and supports, and the importance of self-care and help-seeking, boys can be better equipped to navigate the challenges of adolescence and beyond.

However, mental health literacy is not just about acquiring knowledge - it's also about challenging the stigma and stereotypes that often prevent boys and men from seeking help. Boys may feel pressure to conform to traditional masculine norms of stoicism, self-reliance, and emotional suppression, which can make it difficult to admit when they're struggling and reach out for support.

By promoting mental health literacy and normalizing conversations about mental health, we can create a culture where boys feel empowered to prioritize their well-being and access the resources they need to thrive. This requires a collective effort from parents, educators, healthcare providers, and society as a whole to provide accurate information, reduce stigma, and create supportive environments that foster mental health and resilience."

PROMOTING MENTAL HEALTH IN YOUR DAILY LIFE

In addition to seeking help when needed, there are many ways to promote mental health and wellness in your daily life as a teenage boy, including:

- Practice self-compassion: Self-compassion reduces self-criticism, shame, and feelings of inadequacy, promoting emotional resilience and a more positive self-image.

- Cultivate gratitude: Regularly practicing gratitude can increase positive emotions, life satisfaction, and overall well-being while reducing symptoms of depression and anxiety.
- Set realistic goals: Setting and working towards achievable goals provides a sense of direction, purpose, and accomplishment, boosting self-esteem and motivation.
- Engage in hobbies and interests: Participating in enjoyable activities promotes relaxation, creativity, and a sense of mastery, which can buffer against stress and improve mood.
- Volunteer or give back: Helping others and contributing to your community can provide a sense of meaning, connection, and perspective, promoting mental health and overall well-being.
- Limit social media and screen time: Excessive screen time and social media use can contribute to stress, anxiety, sleep disruption, and negative self-comparison, so setting healthy boundaries is essential for mental well-being.

Remember, promoting mental health and wellness is an ongoing journey that requires patience, self-awareness, and a willingness to try new strategies and seek support when needed. By prioritizing your mental health as a teenage boy, you're setting a strong foundation for a fulfilling and resilient life.

KEY TAKEAWAYS

- Common mental health challenges for teenage boys include depression, anxiety, substance abuse, eating disorders, and trauma-related disorders.
- Experiencing mental health challenges is not a sign of weakness, and seeking help is a sign of strength and self-care.
- Strategies for coping with stress and anxiety include relaxation techniques, regular exercise, adequate sleep, social

support, time management, and challenging negative thoughts.

- Creating a personalized stress management toolbox with helpful techniques and resources can provide a proactive way to handle stress and anxiety.
- Knowing when to seek professional help for persistent or severe mental health symptoms is crucial for well-being and success.
- Mental health literacy involves both knowledge about mental health and challenging stigma and stereotypes that prevent help-seeking.
- Promoting mental health in daily life includes practicing self-compassion, cultivating gratitude, setting realistic goals, engaging in hobbies, volunteering, and limiting excessive screen time.

3

TIME MANAGEMENT AND ORGANIZATION SKILLS

"The key is not to prioritize what's on your schedule, but to schedule your priorities." - Stephen Covey.

As a teenager, you're juggling a lot of responsibilities - school, extracurricular activities, friends, family, and maybe even a part-time job. Therefore, developing strong time management and organizational skills is crucial for teenage boys because:

- It helps you balance the increasing demands and responsibilities of high school, extracurricular activities, social life, and family obligations.
- It reduces stress and anxiety by preventing last-minute rushes and all-nighters.
- It improves your academic performance and grades by ensuring you allocate sufficient time for studying and completing assignments to the best of your abilities.
- It allows you to make time for activities that promote your physical and mental well-being, such as exercise, hobbies, and socializing with friends.

- It sets you up for success in college and future careers, where these skills are essential for managing multiple priorities and deadlines.

THE BENEFITS OF TIME MANAGEMENT

Effective time management can help you:

Reduce stress and anxiety: By creating a schedule and allocating enough time for each task, you can avoid the last-minute rush and the stress that comes with it. For example, if you have a big project due next week, breaking it down into smaller tasks and working on it a little each day can prevent the need for an all-nighter and the associated stress.

Improve your grades and academic performance: When you prioritize your studying and assignments, you're more likely to turn in quality work on time. For instance, if you designate specific hours each day for homework and studying, you'll be better prepared for tests and less likely to miss deadlines, resulting in better grades overall.

Increase your productivity and efficiency: By minimizing distractions and focusing on one task at a time, you can get more done in less time. This can be especially beneficial when you have a lot on your plate, such as during exam week or when you're balancing school with extracurricular activities.

Make time for self-care, hobbies, and relaxation: When you manage your time effectively, you can carve out space for activities that promote your well-being, such as exercise, hobbies, and socializing with friends. For example, if you love playing basketball but struggle to find time for it, scheduling a regular game with friends can ensure that you're making time for the things that matter to you (Scott, 2022).

CREATING A SCHEDULE

One of the most effective ways to manage your time is to create a schedule. Start by listing all of your daily and weekly commitments, such as classes, extracurricular activities, work, and family obligations. Then, block out time for each activity in your calendar or planner.

Be sure to also schedule time for:

- Studying and homework.
- Exercise and physical activity.
- Relaxation and self-care.
- Socializing and hobbies.

EXPERT TIP: THE POMODORO TECHNIQUE

Dr. Jane Smith, a productivity coach, recommends using the Pomodoro Technique for time management:

"One of my favorite time management strategies is the Pomodoro Technique. This involves working on a task for 25 minutes, then taking a 5-minute break. After four 'pomodoros,' take a longer break of 15-30 minutes. This helps you stay focused and avoid burnout by giving your brain regular breaks. It's also a great way to break down large tasks into manageable chunks. I recommend using a timer or app to keep track of your pomodoros."

OVERCOMING PROCRASTINATION

Procrastination is a common challenge for many teenagers. It's easy to put off tasks that seem boring, difficult, or overwhelming. However, procrastination can lead to increased stress, lower grades, and missed opportunities. Here's why overcoming procrastination is so important:

- It helps you avoid the negative consequences of last-minute rushing, such as poor-quality work, increased stress, and potential damage to your reputation or relationships.

- It allows you to break down large, daunting tasks into smaller, manageable steps, making it easier to get started and maintain momentum.
- It enables you to use your time more efficiently and effectively, freeing up space for other important activities and self-care.
- It builds self-discipline, self-trust, and a sense of accomplishment, which can boost your confidence and motivation in all areas of life.

To overcome procrastination, try the following strategies:

- Break large tasks into smaller, more manageable steps.
- Set specific, achievable goals for each study or work session.
- Use positive self-talk and visualization to increase your motivation.
- Reward yourself for completing tasks or reaching milestones.
- Eliminate distractions like social media, TV, or video games during work time.
- Ask for help or support when needed (Lieberman, 2019).

SELF-ASSESSMENT: ARE YOU A PROCRASTINATOR?

Take this quiz to see if you have a tendency to procrastinate:

1. Do you often wait until the last minute to start assignments or projects?

a) Yes

b) No

2. Do you frequently find yourself saying "I'll do it later" or "I work better under pressure"?

a) Yes

b) No

3. Do you often choose short-term pleasures (like watching TV) over long-term goals (like studying for a test)?

a) Yes

b) No

4. Do you tend to underestimate how long tasks will take to complete?

a) Yes

b) No

If you answered "yes" to two or more of these questions, you may have a tendency to procrastinate. Don't worry - with practice and persistence, you can develop better time management habits and overcome procrastination.

STAYING ORGANIZED

In addition to managing your time, it's important to keep your physical and digital spaces organized. A cluttered environment can lead to distraction, stress, and lost time searching for misplaced items. Here's why staying organized is so beneficial:

- It reduces stress and anxiety by creating a sense of order and control in your environment.
- It saves time and energy that would otherwise be wasted searching for lost items or information.
- It improves your ability to focus and be productive, as a clean and organized space minimizes distractions and makes it easier to locate what you need.
- It supports better decision-making and prioritization, as you can quickly assess your commitments and resources.
- It enhances your professional image and reputation, demonstrating responsibility, reliability, and attention to detail.

Some tips for staying organized:

Use a planner or calendar: Keep track of assignments, deadlines, and appointments in one central location. This can help you visualize your week and month, making it easier to plan ahead and avoid double-booking yourself. For example, noting an upcoming test in your planner can remind you to start studying well in advance, rather than cramming at the last minute.

Create a designated study space: Having a clean, organized, and comfortable space to work can improve your focus and productivity. Make sure your study area has good lighting, a comfortable chair, and all the supplies you need close at hand. This can make it easier to sit down and get started on your work, rather than procrastinating or getting distracted by a cluttered environment.

Keep your backpack, locker, and bedroom tidy: Regularly declutter and put items in their proper place. This can save you time and stress in the long run, as you won't have to search for misplaced items or rush to clean up when you have guests over. For instance, keeping your backpack organized can help you quickly find what you need for each class, rather than rummaging through a mess of papers and books.

Use folders, binders, or digital apps: Organize your class notes, handouts, and assignments in a way that makes sense to you. This can make it easier to study for tests, complete homework, and keep track of your progress in each class. For example, using a separate folder or binder for each subject can help you quickly locate the materials you need for a specific class or assignment.

Back up your digital files: Regularly save copies of your important documents, essays, and projects to avoid losing work due to technical issues. This can save you time and stress in the long run, as you won't have to redo lost work or scramble to recreate an assignment at the last minute (Oxford Learning, 2022).

REAL-LIFE STORY: HOW ORGANIZATION HELPED ME SUCCEED

Sam, a high school senior, shares how getting organized transformed his academic performance and stress levels:

"When I started high school, I was constantly losing assignments, missing deadlines, and feeling overwhelmed. My grades started to slip, and I felt like I was always playing catch-up. That's when I realized I needed to get organized.

I started using a planner to keep track of my assignments and extracurricular activities. I also created a filing system for my class notes and handouts so I could easily find what I needed when studying for tests.

At first, it took some extra time and effort to stay organized, but soon it became a habit. My grades started to improve, and I felt much less stressed. I even had more free time for hobbies and socializing because I wasn't wasting time looking for lost items or cramming for tests at the last minute.

Now, as I prepare to graduate and head to college, I know that my organizational skills will be key to my success. I'm confident that I have the tools and habits needed to manage my time, stay on top of my work, and achieve my goals."

KEY TAKEAWAYS

- Effective time management can help reduce stress, improve productivity, and make time for self-care and relaxation.
- Creating a schedule and using techniques like the Pomodoro method can help you prioritize tasks and avoid procrastination.
- Staying organized, both physically and digitally, can save time and reduce stress.
- Developing good time management and organizational habits now will serve you well in college, career, and beyond.

- Remember, time management and organization are skills that take practice and persistence to develop. Be patient with yourself, celebrate your successes, and learn from your challenges. With the right tools and mindset, you can achieve your goals and make the most of your time as a teenager.

4

EFFECTIVE STUDY HABITS AND ACADEMIC SUCCESS STRATEGIES

"There is no substitute for hard work" - Thomas Edison.

Academic success is one of the most important aspects of your teenage years, as it lays the foundation for future educational and career opportunities. Developing strong study habits and academic success strategies is crucial for teenage boys because:

- It helps you learn and retain information more effectively, improving your grades and academic performance.
- It reduces stress and anxiety related to schoolwork and exams by increasing your confidence and preparedness.
- It sets you up for success in higher education and future career pursuits, as the skills you develop now will serve you well in college and beyond.
- It promotes a growth mindset and love of learning, which can enrich your personal and professional life in countless ways.
- It teaches you valuable life skills such as self-discipline, goal-setting, and problem-solving, which are applicable to many areas of life.

IMPROVING MEMORY AND RETENTION

One of the keys to academic success is being able to effectively learn and retain information.

Active recall: Engaging with information through active recall helps strengthen neural connections and moves information from short-term to long-term memory, improving retention and understanding.

Spaced repetition: Spacing out your review sessions helps combat the "forgetting curve" and reinforces learning, leading to better long-term retention and recall of information.

Chunking: Breaking down complex information into smaller, more manageable chunks makes it easier for your brain to process and store the material, improving memory and understanding.

Mnemonic devices: Using memory aids like acronyms, rhymes, or visual associations helps create strong, memorable connections between pieces of information, making it easier to recall later.

EXPERT INSIGHT: THE POWER OF SLEEP FOR MEMORY CONSOLIDATION

Dr. Matthew Walker, a sleep scientist and professor of neuroscience and psychology at the University of California, Berkeley, emphasizes the importance of sleep for memory consolidation:

"Sleep is critical for memory consolidation, which is the process by which newly learned information is transferred from short-term to long-term storage in the brain. During sleep, especially during the deep, non-REM stages, the brain replays and strengthens the neural connections associated with the information you've learned. This is why pulling an all-nighter to study can actually backfire - without adequate sleep, your brain doesn't have the opportunity to properly consolidate and store the information you've been trying to learn" (Walker, 2017).

Another important study skill is taking effective notes during class or while reading. Good note-taking helps you stay engaged with the material, highlight key concepts, and create a valuable resource for later review.

Use the Cornell Method: The Cornell Method helps you organize your notes in a clear, structured way, making it easier to review and study the material later. It also encourages you to synthesize and summarize the information, deepening your understanding.

Focus on main ideas and key details: By focusing on the most important information, you can create more concise, targeted notes that are easier to review and remember without getting bogged down in unnecessary details.

Use abbreviations and symbols: Using shorthand helps you keep up with the pace of a lecture or reading, while still capturing the essential information. This allows you to stay engaged and focused on understanding the material.

Review and revise: Reviewing your notes shortly after class or a reading session helps reinforce your learning and identify any gaps in your understanding. This allows you to seek clarification and fill in missing pieces while the information is still fresh.

REAL-LIFE EXAMPLE: HOW EFFECTIVE NOTE-TAKING HELPED ME ACE MY HISTORY CLASS

Jenny, a high school senior, shares how using the Cornell Method for note-taking helped her succeed in a challenging history class:

"I had always struggled with history, finding it difficult to keep track of all the dates, names, and events we were learning about. But when I started using the Cornell Method for taking notes, it made a huge difference.

Dividing my notes into key words, main ideas, and a summary section helped me organize the information in a way that made sense to me. I would jot down important dates or names in the key word column, write more detailed notes in the main section, and then summarize the main points at the bottom of the page.

When it came time to study for tests, I had a clear, concise set of notes to review, with key information easily accessible. I also used the keyword column to quiz myself and identify areas where I needed more review.

Using this note-taking method, along with other study strategies like active recall and spaced repetition, I was able to raise my history grade from a C to an A-. More importantly, I actually started to enjoy learning about history and felt more confident in my ability to understand and retain complex information."

PREPARING FOR EXAMS

Exams are a major part of academic life, and knowing how to prepare effectively can make a big difference in your performance and stress levels.

Start early: Starting your exam preparation well in advance gives you time to thoroughly review the material, identify areas of weakness, and seek help if needed, reducing last-minute stress and improving performance.

Create a study schedule: Breaking your exam preparation into manageable chunks and creating a schedule helps you stay organized, motivated, and on track, ensuring that you allocate sufficient time for each subject or topic.

Identify and focus on key concepts: By focusing your studying on the most important concepts and ideas, you can prioritize your time and energy effectively, increasing your understanding and retention of the material.

Practice active recall: Engaging in active recall activities like quizzing, creating practice problems, or teaching others helps reinforce your learning, identify gaps in your understanding, and improve your ability to apply the information in new contexts.

Take care of yourself: Taking care of your physical and mental health is essential for optimal cognitive function and academic performance. Getting enough sleep, eating well, and managing stress can help you stay focused, motivated, and resilient during exams.

SEEKING HELP WHEN NEEDED

An important part of academic success is knowing when to ask for help. Seeking help is so important because:

- It allows you to clarify confusing concepts, fill in gaps in your understanding, and learn from the expertise of others.
- It helps you overcome obstacles and challenges that may be hindering your academic progress.
- It promotes a growth mindset and understanding that asking for help is a sign of strength and commitment to learning, not weakness.
- It builds relationships with teachers, tutors, and peers, who can provide ongoing support and encouragement in your academic journey.

Remember, asking for help is a sign of strength, not weakness. It shows that you are proactive about your learning and committed to your academic success.

KEY TAKEAWAYS

- Improving memory and retention involves active recall, spaced repetition, chunking, and mnemonic devices.
- Taking effective notes using strategies like the Cornell Method can help you organize information and create a valuable study resource.
- Preparing for exams requires starting early, creating a study schedule, focusing on key concepts, practicing active recall, and taking care of your physical and mental health.

- Seeking help from teachers, tutors, or classmates when needed is an important part of academic success.

5

GOAL SETTING AND DECISION-MAKING

"The only limit to the height of your achievements is the reach of your dreams and your willingness to work for them" – Michelle Obama.

As a teenager, you are at a critical juncture in your life where the decisions you make and the goals you set can have a profound impact on your future.

- It helps you clarify your values, priorities, and aspirations, giving you a sense of direction and purpose.
- It enables you to take control of your life and actively shape your future rather than simply reacting to circumstances.
- It builds confidence, motivation, and resilience by providing a framework for overcoming challenges and achieving success.
- It prepares you for the increasing responsibilities and complexities of adulthood, both personally and professionally.
- It allows you to make informed, intentional choices that align with your long-term goals and well-being.

SETTING SMART GOALS AS A TEEN

One of the most powerful tools for setting and achieving goals is the SMART criteria. SMART is an acronym that stands for Specific, Measurable, Achievable, Relevant, and Time-bound.

- Specific goals provide clarity and focus, making it easier to understand what you need to do and how to get there.
- Measurable goals allow you to track your progress, celebrate your successes, and adjust your approach as needed.
- Achievable goals strike a balance between being challenging and realistic, keeping you motivated without setting you up for disappointment.
- Relevant goals align with your larger values and priorities, ensuring that you're investing your time and energy in things that matter to you.
- Time-bound goals create a sense of urgency and accountability, helping you stay on track and avoid procrastination.

REAL-LIFE EXAMPLE: AIDEN'S ACADEMIC GOAL

Aiden, a 16-year-old high school student, was struggling to maintain his grades in math. He knew he needed to improve his performance, but he wasn't sure how to set an effective goal. Using the SMART criteria, Aiden developed the following goal:

"I will raise my math grade from a C to a B by the end of the semester by attending tutoring sessions twice a week and completing all my homework assignments on time."

Let's break down how Aiden's goal meets the SMART criteria:

- Specific: Aiden clearly states what he wants to achieve (raise his math grade from a C to a B) and how he plans to do it (attending tutoring sessions and completing homework on time).

- Measurable: Aiden's goal is measurable, as he can track his progress by monitoring his grades and homework completion.
- Achievable: While challenging, Aiden's goal is realistic and attainable through dedicated effort and support from tutoring.
- Relevant: Improving his math grade is relevant to Aiden's overall academic success and future aspirations.
- Time-bound: Aiden has set a specific deadline for achieving his goal (the end of the semester), which creates a sense of urgency and accountability.

By setting a SMART goal, Aiden was able to focus his efforts, track his progress, and ultimately improve his math grade. This experience taught him the power of effective goal-setting and how it can be applied to various areas of his life.

THE DECISION-MAKING PROCESS: A STEP-BY-STEP GUIDE

In addition to setting goals, teenagers also face many important decisions that can have lasting impacts on their lives. Here's why having a structured decision-making process is so valuable:

- It helps you approach decisions systematically and thoroughly, considering all relevant factors and perspectives.
- It reduces the influence of impulsivity, bias, or external pressure by providing a logical framework for evaluating options.
- It increases your chances of making choices that align with your goals, values, and long-term best interests.
- It builds your confidence and decision-making skills over time, preparing you for increasingly complex and consequential decisions in the future.

To make sound decisions, it's helpful to have a framework or process to follow. Here is a step-by-step guide to effective decision-making:

Step 1: Identify the decision to be made. Start by clarifying the choice you need to make and why it's important. What are the potential consequences or outcomes of this decision? Who else might be affected by it?

Step 2: Gather information. Once you have a clear understanding of the decision at hand, start collecting relevant information to help you weigh your options. This might include researching potential paths, seeking advice from trusted mentors, or reflecting on your own values and priorities.

Step 3: Weigh the options. With the necessary information in hand, evaluate the pros and cons of each potential choice. Consider factors like short-term and long-term consequences, alignment with your goals and values, and potential risks or obstacles.

Step 4: Make the decision. Based on your analysis, choose the option that best aligns with your goals and priorities. Trust your instincts, but also be open to input from others who may have valuable perspectives to share.

Step 5: Take action. Once you've made your decision, commit to it and take the necessary steps to follow through. This might involve creating a plan, enlisting support from others, or breaking the goal down into smaller, manageable tasks.

Step 6: Evaluate the outcome. After you've implemented your decision, take time to reflect on the results. Did things turn out as you hoped? What did you learn from the experience? Use this feedback to inform future decisions and adjust your approach as needed.

By following these steps, you can approach decisions in a structured and thoughtful way, increasing your chances of making choices that align with your goals and values. Let's take a look at how this process can be applied to a real-life situation.

REAL-LIFE EXAMPLE: JACKSON'S CAREER PATH DECISION

Jackson, a 17-year-old high school senior, was unsure about what career path to pursue after graduation. He had always been interested in both engineering and business but struggled to decide which to study in college. Using the decision-making process, Jackson approached his dilemma systematically:

Step 1: Jackson identified his decision: choosing between studying engineering or business in college.

Step 2: He researched both fields, spoke with professionals in each industry, and sought guidance from his school's career counselor.

Step 3: Jackson weighed the pros and cons of each path, considering factors such as job prospects, salary potential, and alignment with his skills and interests.

Step 4: Based on his analysis, Jackson decided to pursue a degree in engineering with a minor in business. This path would allow him to combine his technical skills with his entrepreneurial spirit.

Step 5: Jackson took action by applying to engineering programs and seeking out internships and mentorship opportunities in the field.

Step 6: Throughout his college journey, Jackson regularly reflected on his decision and made adjustments as needed, such as taking additional business classes to enhance his skills.

By following a structured decision-making process, Jackson was able to approach a major life decision with clarity and confidence, setting himself up for success in his future career.

OVERCOMING INDECISION: TOOLS AND TECHNIQUES FOR TEENS

Even with a clear decision-making process, many teens struggle with indecision at times. Learning to overcome indecision is so important because:

- It helps you avoid the stress, anxiety, and paralysis that can come from prolonged uncertainty or ambivalence.
- It enables you to seize opportunities and take action toward your goals rather than getting stuck in a cycle of deliberation.
- It builds your confidence and trust in your own judgment, reducing the need for constant reassurance or validation from others.
- It frees up mental and emotional energy for other important aspects of your life, such as relationships, personal growth, and self-care.

If you find yourself struggling with indecision, there are several tools and techniques you can use to gain clarity and confidence:

Decision matrices: Create a grid with potential options on one axis and key decision criteria on the other. Rate each option on a scale for each criterion, then tally up the scores to see which choice comes out on top.

Pros and cons lists: For each option, brainstorm a list of potential benefits and drawbacks. See which choice has the most compelling upsides and the most manageable downsides.

Scenario planning: Imagine yourself pursuing each potential path and envision what your life might look like in the short-term and long-term. Which scenario feels most aligned with your goals and values?

Intuition checks: While it's important to approach decisions rationally, don't discount the role of intuition or gut feelings. If one choice just feels right, even if you can't fully explain why, that's often a sign that it aligns with your deepest values and priorities.

INTERACTIVE ACTIVITY: GOAL-SETTING WORKSHOP

To put your goal-setting skills into practice, try this interactive workshop:

1. Identify an area of your life where you'd like to set a goal, such as academics, health and fitness, personal growth, or relationships.

2. Write down a draft goal statement for this area, focusing on what you want to achieve.

3. Evaluate your draft goal against the SMART criteria:

- Is it Specific? Does it clearly state what you want to accomplish?
- Is it Measurable? Can you track your progress and know when you've achieved it?
- Is it Achievable? Is it challenging but still realistic, given your current resources and circumstances?
- Is it Relevant? Does it align with your larger values and priorities?
- Is it Time-bound? Have you set a clear deadline for achieving the goal?

4. If your draft goal doesn't meet all the SMART criteria, revise it until it does. Keep refining your goal statement until you have a clear, focused, and actionable target.

5. Once you have a SMART goal, break it down into smaller, manageable steps. Create a timeline for completing each step, and identify any resources or support you'll need along the way.

6. Share your goal with a trusted friend, family member, or mentor. Ask them to check in with you regularly to provide accountability and encouragement.

7. As you work towards your goal, keep track of your progress and celebrate your successes along the way. If you encounter obstacles or setbacks, use them as opportunities to learn and adjust your approach.

By practicing goal-setting in a structured way, you'll develop a valuable skill that you can apply to all areas of your life. Remember, setting effective goals is not about perfection but about progress and growth. With time and practice, you'll become more confident and skilled at creating and achieving meaningful goals for yourself.

LEARNING FROM FAILURE: HOW TO BOUNCE BACK STRONGER

No matter how carefully you plan or how thoroughly you weigh your options, there will be times when your decisions don't lead to the desired outcomes. Learning to embrace and learn from failure is so crucial:

- It helps you develop resilience, adaptability, and a growth mindset, which are essential for long-term success and well-being.
- It provides valuable lessons and insights that can inform your future goals, decisions, and strategies.
- It normalizes the experience of setbacks and challenges, reducing the fear and shame that can hold you back from taking risks or trying new things.
- It cultivates humility, empathy, and a willingness to learn from others, strengthening your relationships and leadership skills.

EXPERT INSIGHT: THE POWER OF A GROWTH MINDSET

Dr. Carol Dweck, a renowned psychologist and author of "Mindset: The New Psychology of Success," highlights the importance of adopting a growth mindset in the face of failure:

"In a growth mindset, people believe that their most basic abilities can be developed through dedication and hard work - brains and talent are just the starting point. This view creates a love of learning and a resilience that is

essential for great accomplishment. Virtually all great people have had these qualities."

By approaching failure with a growth mindset - seeing it as an opportunity to learn, develop, and improve - you can cultivate the resilience and persistence needed to achieve your long-term goals. Instead of being discouraged by setbacks, you'll be motivated to try again, armed with new insights and strategies.

THE IMPORTANCE OF FLEXIBILITY IN PLANNING YOUR FUTURE

As a teenager, it's natural to feel pressure to have your entire future mapped out. But the reality is that life is full of unexpected twists and turns, and the best-laid plans often go awry. Cultivating flexibility and adaptability is so important because:

- It allows you to take advantage of unexpected opportunities and experiences that may enrich your personal or professional journey.
- It helps you navigate the inevitable challenges, changes, and uncertainties of life with greater ease and resilience.
- It enables you to stay true to yourself and your evolving interests, values, and goals rather than feeling locked into a rigid plan.
- It fosters a sense of curiosity, open-mindedness, and continuous learning, which are valuable assets in any field or endeavor.

REAL-LIFE EXAMPLE: EMILY'S EVOLVING PASSIONS

Emily, a 16-year-old high school student, had always dreamed of becoming a professional dancer. She had been dancing since she was three years old and had dedicated countless hours to training and practice. However, during her sophomore year, Emily discovered a new passion: writing.

At first, Emily was hesitant to explore this new interest, afraid that it would distract her from her dance goals. But with encouragement from her English teacher, she began submitting her work to writing contests and literary magazines. To her surprise, she started receiving recognition for her writing, including a prestigious award from a national organization.

As Emily delved deeper into the world of writing, she realized that her love for storytelling and creativity could be expressed in many different ways. She began to see her future in a new light - one that included both dance and writing.

With the support of her family and mentors, Emily decided to pursue a double major in dance and creative writing in college. She knew it would be challenging to balance both passions, but she also recognized the value of having multiple avenues for expressing herself and making an impact.

Through this experience, Emily learned the importance of staying open to new possibilities and being willing to adapt her plans as her interests and circumstances evolved. By cultivating a flexible and curious mindset, she was able to discover new facets of herself and create a future path that truly resonated with her passions and values.

KEY TAKEAWAYS

- Goal-setting and decision-making are two of the most important skills you can develop as a teenager, as they will serve you well in all areas of your life, from education and career to personal relationships and well-being.
- Using the SMART criteria can help you set effective goals that are challenging yet attainable, and that align with your values and aspirations.
- Following a clear decision-making process, including identifying the decision, gathering information, weighing options, making the choice, taking action, and evaluating the

outcome, can help you approach decisions with greater clarity, confidence, and intentionality.

- Overcoming indecision may involve using tools like decision matrices, pros and cons lists, scenario planning, and intuition checks, as well as practicing decisiveness in low-stakes situations.
- Failure is a natural and inevitable part of the learning process, and reframing it as an opportunity for growth and improvement can help you develop resilience and extract valuable lessons from setbacks.
- Cultivating flexibility and adaptability is crucial in planning for the future, as life is full of unexpected twists and turns. Staying open to new experiences, building backup plans, and reframing challenges as opportunities can help you navigate change with greater ease and resourcefulness.

By developing strong goal-setting and decision-making skills as a teenager, you'll be well-equipped to create a life that is authentic, fulfilling, and true to who you are. Remember, your future is an ongoing journey of growth, learning, and self-discovery - embrace the process and trust in your own potential.

6

DIGITAL LITERACY: NAVIGATING THE ONLINE WORLD

"The internet is becoming the town square for the global village of tomorrow"- Bill Gates.

In today's digital age, being digitally literate is more important than ever, especially for teenage boys who are growing up in a world increasingly shaped by technology.

- It helps you stay safe online by protecting your personal information, avoiding scams and predators, and knowing how to handle cyberbullying or other digital threats.
- It enables you to build and maintain a positive online reputation, which can impact your future educational and career opportunities.
- It allows you to critically evaluate the information you encounter online, distinguishing between reliable sources and fake news or propaganda.
- It empowers you to use technology in a way that benefits you and society rather than causing harm or perpetuating negative behaviors.

- It prepares you for success in a world where digital skills are increasingly essential for communication, collaboration, and innovation.

ONLINE SAFETY AND PRIVACY

One of the biggest challenges of the digital world is protecting your personal information and staying safe online. It's essential to be aware of the potential risks and take steps to protect yourself because:

- Using strong, unique passwords helps prevent hackers from gaining access to your accounts and personal information.
- Being cautious about sharing personal information online reduces your risk of identity theft, scams, and other digital threats.
- Keeping your social media profiles private and only accepting friend requests from people you know in real life helps you control who has access to your personal information and posts.
- Being aware of the signs of cyberbullying and knowing how to report it empowers you to take action against online harassment and protect yourself and others.
- Using privacy settings allows you to control who can see your posts and information, giving you greater control over your online presence.

EXPERT TIP: CREATING STRONG PASSWORDS

John Daw, a cybersecurity expert, advises on creating secure passwords:

"One of the most important things you can do to protect your online accounts is to use strong, unique passwords. A strong password should be at least 12 characters long and include a mix of uppercase and lowercase letters, numbers, and symbols. Avoid using personal information like your birthdate or pet's name, and never use the same password for multiple accounts.

Consider using a password manager to help you generate and store complex passwords securely."

DIGITAL FOOTPRINT AND REPUTATION

Everything you do online leaves a digital footprint, which can have a significant impact on your reputation and future opportunities. This is why managing your digital footprint is so important:

- Potential employers, colleges, and others may make decisions about your future based on what they find about you online.
- Posting inappropriate or offensive content can damage your reputation and relationships, even years later.
- Taking control of your online presence allows you to showcase your accomplishments, interests, and values in a positive light.
- Building a positive digital footprint can open up new opportunities and connections that align with your goals and passions.

REAL-LIFE STORY: THE CONSEQUENCES OF A NEGATIVE DIGITAL FOOTPRINT

Ryan, a high school senior, shares how his online activity impacted his college admission:

"I was excited to apply to my dream college. I had good grades, strong test scores, and an impressive list of extracurricular activities. However, when the college admissions officer googled my name, they found some concerning content.

I had posted photos of myself at parties drinking alcohol and using inappropriate language on social media. I had also engaged in online arguments and made insensitive comments about certain groups of people. The admissions officer was concerned about my judgment and maturity and ultimately decided not to offer me admission to the college.

I was devastated and wished I had been more mindful of my online presence. I learned the hard way that what you post online can have real-life consequences, even years later."

MEDIA LITERACY AND FAKE NEWS

In the age of social media and 24/7 news cycles, it's more important than ever to be able to distinguish between reliable information and fake news. Media literacy is the ability to critically evaluate and analyze the media messages you encounter, whether it's a news article, social media post, or advertisement (Steele, 2021).

SOME STRATEGIES FOR IMPROVING YOUR MEDIA LITERACY:

- Check the source: is it a reputable news outlet or a questionable website?
- Look for multiple sources reporting the same information.
- Be skeptical of sensational headlines or stories that seem too good (or bad) to be true.
- Watch out for biased language or one-sided reporting.
- Use fact-checking websites like Snopes or PolitiFact to verify information (Gebel, 2020).

INTERACTIVE ACTIVITY: SPOT THE FAKE NEWS

Let's practice your media literacy skills. Read the following news headlines and decide whether you think they are real or fake:

1. "NASA Confirms Earth Will Experience 15 Days of Darkness in November 2023".

2. "New Study Finds Drinking Coffee Reduces Risk of Cancer by 50%".

3. "President Signs Bill to Eliminate All Student Loan Debt".

4. "Scientists Discover New Species of Dinosaur in Antarctica".

Answers:

1. Fake - This is a recurring fake news story that has been circulating for years. NASA has confirmed it is not true.

2. Real - While the specific percentage may vary, there have been studies suggesting a link between coffee consumption and lower risk of certain cancers.

3. Fake - As of 2023, no such bill has been signed into law. Be cautious of news that seems too good to be true.

4. Real - In 2020, scientists did discover a new species of dinosaur in Antarctica based on fossil evidence. Always check the source and date of news stories to verify their accuracy.

DIGITAL CITIZENSHIP AND ONLINE ETIQUETTE

As a digital citizen, you have both rights and responsibilities when it comes to your online behavior. Practicing good digital citizenship is important because:

- It creates a more positive, respectful, and inclusive online community for everyone.
- It protects your own privacy and reputation, as well as the privacy and well-being of others.
- It promotes the use of technology for good rather than harm or exploitation.
- It prepares you to be a responsible, ethical leader in a digital world.

SELF-REFLECTION: ASSESSING YOUR DIGITAL CITIZENSHIP

Take a moment to reflect on your own digital citizenship. Ask yourself the following questions:

1. Do I always treat others with kindness and respect online, even if I disagree with them?

2. Do I ask permission before posting photos or information about others online?

3. Do I give credit to the original creator when sharing content online?

4. Do I report cyberbullying or online hate speech when I see it?

5. Do I use technology in a way that benefits myself and society rather than causing harm?

If you answered "no" to any of these questions, consider what steps you can take to become a better digital citizen. Remember, your online actions have real-world consequences, so always strive to be a positive force in the digital community.

THE IMPACT OF TECHNOLOGY ON MENTAL HEALTH

While technology can be a great tool for staying connected and informed, it can also have negative impacts on our mental health if not used in moderation. Here's why it's important to be mindful of your technology use:

- Comparing yourself to others on social media can lead to feelings of inadequacy, anxiety, and depression.
- Excessive screen time, especially before bed, can disrupt your sleep and negatively impact your mood and cognitive function.
- Addiction to social media or gaming can interfere with your relationships, responsibilities, and overall well-being.
- Cyberbullying and other negative online interactions can cause significant emotional distress and trauma.

KEY TAKEAWAYS

To protect your mental health in the digital age, try to:

- Limit your screen time, especially before bed.
- Be mindful of how social media makes you feel and take breaks if needed.
- Engage in offline activities and hobbies that bring you joy and fulfillment.
- Seek support from friends, family, or a mental health professional if you're struggling (National Alliance on Mental Illness, 2022).
- Protect your personal information and stay safe online by using strong passwords, being cautious about sharing information, and knowing how to report cyberbullying.
- Be mindful of your digital footprint and take steps to build a positive online presence.
- Develop media literacy skills to critically evaluate the information you encounter online.
- Practice good digital citizenship by being responsible, respectful, and ethical in your online interactions.
- Too much screen time and technology use can lead to anxiety, depression, and other mental health challenges.
- To protect your mental health, limit your screen time, engage in offline activities, and seek support if needed.

By being mindful of how technology impacts your relationships and mental health, you can use it in a way that enhances your life and connections with others. Remember, technology is a tool, not a replacement for real-life interactions and experiences.

7

SELF-CARE AND PERSONAL HYGIENE

"Take care of your body. It's the only place you have to live" -
Jim Rohn

Hey there! As a teenage guy, it's super important to take care of yourself. This means eating right, exercising, getting enough sleep, and keeping yourself clean. Taking care of yourself isn't just about looking good - it's about feeling good and being healthy, too.

WHY SELF-CARE MATTERS

Self-care is all about developing habits that will keep you physically, mentally, and emotionally healthy, now and in the future. When you make self-care a priority, you can:

Grow and develop in a healthy way during your teenage years.

Build habits that will keep you from getting sick or having health problems later on.

Feel better, have a better mood, and deal with stress and challenges more easily.

Feel more confident and good about yourself overall.

Set yourself up to do well in school, in relationships, and in your future career.

EATING RIGHT

Eating a balanced, healthy diet is really important for supporting your growth, development, and energy levels.

Your body needs different nutrients, like proteins, carbs, healthy fats, vitamins, and minerals, to work its best and support your growing body.

Eating right helps you stay at a healthy weight, keeps you from getting chronic diseases, and supports your mental health and brain function.

Eating regular, balanced meals helps keep your energy levels, mood, and focus steady throughout the day.

Here are some tips for eating better:

- Eat different kinds of foods: Include lots of fruits, veggies, whole grains, lean proteins, and healthy fats in your diet to make sure you're getting all the nutrients you need.
- Go easy on junk food: Cut back on sugary drinks, snacks, and fast food, which can make you gain weight, get cavities, and have other health issues.
- Drink lots of water: Drink plenty of water throughout the day to keep your body working right and to stay healthy. Try to drink at least 8 cups (64 ounces) of water per day.
- Don't skip meals: Eating regular, balanced meals helps keep your energy levels up and supports healthy growth and development. Try to eat three main meals a day and healthy snacks if you need them.

MIKE'S STORY: EATING RIGHT FOR SPORTS

Mike, a 16-year-old soccer player, talks about how he learned how important good nutrition is for playing sports:

"I used to think that as long as I was training hard, I could eat whatever I wanted. But I started feeling tired during practices and games. My coach said I should look at my diet. I did some research and realized I wasn't giving my body the fuel it needed to perform at its best.

I started making changes like eating a balanced breakfast, packing healthy snacks, and choosing healthier options. I noticed a difference in my energy levels and performance almost right away. I felt stronger, faster, and more focused on the field.

Now, I make nutrition a priority as part of my overall training plan. I know that what I put into my body directly impacts how well I perform in sports and how healthy I am overall."

GETTING MOVING

Regular exercise is important for staying healthy, managing stress, and supporting your physical and mental development. Here's why:

Exercise helps you stay at a healthy weight, builds strong bones and muscles, and improves heart health.

Being physically active releases endorphins, which make you feel better and reduce stress and anxiety.

Regular exercise can give you more energy, help you sleep better, and improve your brain function and performance in school.

Experts recommend that teenagers get at least 60 minutes of medium to hard exercise each day, including a mix of aerobic activity and strength training.

Tips for making exercise part of your daily routine:

Find activities you like: Choose physical activities that you enjoy, like playing a sport, going for a run, or taking a dance class. This will make it easier to stick with a regular exercise routine.

Make it social: Working out with friends or joining a team can make exercise more fun and give you support and accountability.

Set goals and track your progress: Having specific goals you can reach can help motivate you to stay active. Track your progress using a fitness app or journal.

Be active throughout the day: Look for ways to be active during the day, like walking or biking to school, taking the stairs, or doing body-weight exercises during study breaks.

GETTING ENOUGH SLEEP

Getting enough good quality sleep is super important for your physical health, mental well-being, and success in school.

Sleep lets your body and brain rest, repair, and grow, which is especially important during your teenage years.

Getting enough sleep supports learning, memory, and doing well in school.

Not getting enough sleep can lead to mood problems, less motivation, trouble making decisions, and taking more risks.

Experts recommend that teenagers aged 14-17 get 8-10 hours of sleep per night.

TIPS TO SLEEP BETTER AND LONGER:

Stick to a sleep schedule: Try to go to bed and wake up at the same time every day, even on weekends. This helps regulate your body's internal clock and improves the quality of your sleep.

Have a relaxing bedtime routine: Do calm activities like reading, stretching, or writing in a journal before bed to let your body know it's time to sleep.

Cut back on screen time before bed: The blue light from phones, tablets, and computers can mess with your body's natural sleep-wake cycle. Try to avoid screens for at least an hour before bedtime.

Create a sleep-friendly space: Keep your bedroom dark, quiet, and cool to help you sleep better. Invest in a comfortable mattress and pillows to support your body and reduce discomfort.

EXPERT TIP: WHAT HAPPENS WHEN YOU DON'T GET ENOUGH SLEEP

Dr. Judith Owens, a sleep expert at Boston Children's Hospital, talks about how important sleep is for teenagers' health and well-being:

"Not getting enough sleep over time can have serious consequences for teenagers' physical and mental health, as well as their performance in school and safety. Not getting enough sleep is linked to a higher risk of obesity, diabetes, heart disease, depression, anxiety, and substance abuse, as well as problems with thinking, making decisions, and reaction time. This can lead to trouble in school, problems in relationships, and even a higher risk of accidents and injuries.

It's really important for teenagers to make getting enough good quality sleep a priority every night. This means sticking to a regular sleep schedule, having a relaxing bedtime routine, and limiting exposure to screens and stimulating activities before bed. If you're having trouble sleeping or feeling really tired during the day, talk to your doctor or a sleep specialist to rule out any sleep disorders and come up with a plan for improving your sleep."

KEEPING CLEAN

Keeping yourself clean is important for both your health and your social interactions. Here's why:

- Good hygiene habits help stop the spread of germs, bacteria, and illnesses.
- Keeping clean can reduce body odor, skin irritation, and dental problems.
- Looking and smelling clean can make you feel more confident and accepted by others.

As a teenage guy, it's especially important to develop consistent hygiene habits to deal with changes like sweating more and having more body odor. Some basic hygiene tips:

Shower or bathe regularly: Try to shower or bathe at least once a day, using soap and warm water to clean your skin and hair. Pay extra attention to areas like your armpits, groin, and feet, which tend to sweat and smell more.

Use deodorant or antiperspirant: Put on deodorant or antiperspirant every day to control body odor and sweat. If you sweat a lot, think about using a stronger antiperspirant.

Wash your face twice a day: Use a gentle cleanser and warm water to wash your face in the morning and before bed. This can help prevent acne breakouts and keep your skin looking clean and healthy.

Brush and floss your teeth: Brush your teeth twice a day for two minutes each time, using toothpaste with fluoride. Floss every day to remove plaque and food particles from between your teeth and along your gum line.

Wear clean clothes: Change out of sweaty or dirty clothes as soon as you can, and try to wear clean clothes every day. Wash your clothes, including socks and underwear, regularly to prevent odor and bacteria growth.

WHAT DRESSING FOR SUCCESS MEANS FOR TEENAGERS

As a teenage guy, understanding how to dress appropriately for different occasions is an important life skill. The way you present yourself through your clothing and grooming choices can affect how others see you and how confident you feel in different settings. Here are some key tips for dressing for success:

Know the dress codes: Learn about common dress codes (e.g., casual, business casual, formal) and what they usually mean. This knowledge will help you choose the right outfits for different events or situations, like job interviews, school presentations, or family gatherings.

Get some versatile, quality basics: Build your wardrobe with classic, versatile pieces that you can mix and match easily, like dark wash jeans, neutral t-shirts, button-down shirts, and a blazer or sports coat that fits well. Choose quality over quantity so your clothes last longer and look better over time.

Make sure your clothes fit: Clothes that fit well are key for looking polished and put-together. Make sure your clothes aren't too tight or too loose, and get them tailored if you need to. Pay special attention to how suits, dress shirts, and pants fit, since these pieces can have a big impact on how you look overall.

Take care of your appearance: Good hygiene and grooming habits are just as important as your clothing choices. Shower every day, use deodorant, brush your teeth, and keep your hair clean and styled. Getting regular haircuts, keeping your nails trimmed, and shaving or maintaining facial hair can also help you look more polished.

Dress for the occasion: When choosing an outfit, always think about the specific event or situation you're dressing for. A job interview might require a more formal, conservative look, while hanging out with friends allows for more relaxed, expressive clothing choices. If you're not sure, it's usually better to be a little overdressed than underdressed.

By following these guidelines and developing your own personal style over time, you'll be well-equipped to dress for success in any situation. Remember, the goal is to feel confident, comfortable, and appropriate in your clothing choices so you can focus on making the most of every opportunity that comes your way.

FIRST IMPRESSIONS COUNT

Whether you're meeting someone for the first time, going to a job interview, or giving a presentation in class, how you look plays a big role in how others see you. Studies have shown that people form impressions within the first few seconds of meeting someone, and what you're wearing is a key factor in shaping those impressions.

MARCUS'S INTERVIEW STORY

Marcus, a 17-year-old high school student, had always been interested in technology and was thrilled when he got an interview for a summer internship at a local tech startup. He knew this was a valuable opportunity to get experience and make connections in the industry.

On the day of the interview, Marcus put on his favorite t-shirt and jeans, thinking the casual clothes would reflect the laid-back culture of the startup. However, when he arrived at the office, he noticed that everyone else was dressed in business casual attire, making him feel underdressed and out of place.

During the interview, Marcus felt self-conscious about his appearance and had trouble focusing on the questions being asked. He left the interview feeling that he hadn't made the best impression and worried that his clothes might have cost him the opportunity.

A few days later, Marcus got an email from the startup thanking him for his interest but saying they had chosen another candidate for the internship. While he couldn't be sure, Marcus couldn't help but wonder if his casual attire had played a role in the decision.

This experience taught Marcus how important it is to research a company's culture and dress appropriately for the occasion. He realized that even in a more casual industry like tech, it's essential to present yourself in a way that shows you're serious about the opportunity and respect the company's values.

FINDING YOUR STYLE

Developing a personal style that reflects who you are and what you value is an important part of dressing for success. Your style should make you feel confident, comfortable, and like yourself, while still being appropriate for the occasion.

Some tips for finding your style:

Know what you like: Think about the colors, patterns, and styles you're naturally drawn to and that make you feel good about yourself.

Dress for your body type: Choose clothes that fit well and look good on your body shape, rather than just following trends that may not work for you.

Try new things: Don't be afraid to experiment with different styles and combinations until you find what works best for you.

Get versatile pieces: Look for clothes that can be dressed up or down and worn in different settings, like a classic blazer or dark wash jeans.

TAKING CARE OF YOUR CLOTHES

Taking care of your clothes is a key part of dressing for success. Not only does it help your clothes last longer, but it also makes sure you always look your best. Some basic skills for taking care of your clothes include:

Reading and following care labels: Pay attention to the specific instructions for washing, drying, and ironing each piece of clothing.

Storing clothes properly: Hang or fold clothes neatly to prevent wrinkles and damage. Use hangers for items that might stretch out of shape, like sweaters or dress shirts.

Treating stains quickly: Act fast when spills happen, and use the right cleaning methods for different types of stains (e.g. blotting vs. rubbing).

Investing in quality: While you don't need to spend a ton of money, buying a few well-made, versatile pieces can be more cost-effective in the long run than buying cheaper, lower-quality items that need to be replaced often.

Remember, dressing for success isn't about following strict rules or trying to be someone you're not. It's about understanding how your appearance can influence how others see you and the opportunities you get and presenting yourself in a way that reflects your best self. By developing your personal style, dressing appropriately for different occasions, and taking care of your clothes, you'll be well on your way to making a positive impression and achieving your goals.

KEY TAKEAWAYS

- Eating a balanced, healthy diet that includes different types of foods, limits processed and sugary items, and focuses on regular meals can support teenage guys' growth, development, and energy levels.
- Regular exercise, including a mix of cardio and strength training, is important for physical and mental health.
- Getting enough good quality sleep, aiming for 8-10 hours per night, is crucial for overall well-being and doing well in school.
- Developing consistent hygiene habits like showering regularly, using deodorant, washing your face, brushing and flossing, and wearing clean clothes is important for health and social well-being.
- First impressions count, and what you wear plays a big role in how others see you. Developing a personal style that reflects who you are and what you value, dressing appropriately for different occasions, and taking care of your clothes are key for dressing for success and building confidence.

8

THE IMPACT OF TECHNOLOGY ON RELATIONSHIPS

"Technology is just a tool. In terms of getting the kids working together and motivating them, the teacher is the most important" – Bill Gates.

Technology has changed the way we connect and communicate with others, especially for your generation of digital natives. Here's why it's crucial to understand the impact of technology on relationships:

- It can help you build and maintain connections with friends and family, even across long distances or busy schedules.
- It can also lead to misunderstandings, hurt feelings, or distractions if not used mindfully and in moderation.
- Excessive technology use can contribute to feelings of loneliness, anxiety, depression, and other mental health challenges.
- Understanding the potential benefits and pitfalls of digital communication can help you make informed choices about how to use technology in a way that enhances, rather than detracts from, your relationships and well-being.

THE BENEFITS AND CHALLENGES OF DIGITAL COMMUNICATION

One of the biggest changes brought about by technology is the rise of digital communication, whether it's texting, social media, or video chat. These tools can be a great way to stay connected with friends and family, especially if you live far apart or have busy schedules (Nguyen, 2020).

However, digital communication can also have its challenges. It's easy to misinterpret the tone or meaning of a text message or social media post, which can lead to misunderstandings or hurt feelings. It's also easy to get caught up in the constant stream of notifications and messages, which can be distracting and stressful (Pew Research Center, 2021).

RESEARCH SPOTLIGHT: THE LINK BETWEEN SOCIAL MEDIA AND MENTAL HEALTH

A 2021 study by the American Academy of Pediatrics found that excessive social media use was linked to higher rates of depression, anxiety, and sleep problems in adolescents. The study surveyed over 6,500 teenagers and found that those who spent more than three hours per day on social media were more likely to report mental health issues, compared to those who spent less time online.

The researchers suggest that the constant comparison to others' curated online lives, exposure to cyberbullying, and disrupted sleep patterns may contribute to these negative outcomes. They recommend that parents and caregivers set reasonable limits on screen time and encourage alternative activities like in-person socializing, exercise, and hobbies (Nagata et al., 2021).

BALANCING ONLINE AND OFFLINE INTERACTIONS

While digital communication is important, it's also crucial to maintain face-to-face interactions and build strong, in-person relationships.

In-person interactions provide a deeper sense of connection, empathy, and understanding that can be harder to achieve through screens alone.

Spending too much time online can lead to feelings of loneliness, disconnection, and FOMO (fear of missing out), especially if you're constantly comparing your life to others' curated highlight reels.

Face-to-face communication helps you develop important social skills, like reading nonverbal cues, active listening, and conflict resolution, that are essential for success in personal and professional relationships.

Engaging in offline activities and hobbies can provide a sense of balance, fulfillment, and meaning that complements your online life.

To maintain a healthy balance, try to:

Set aside dedicated time for face-to-face interactions with friends and family.

Limit your screen time, especially before bed or during meals.

Be present and engaged when spending time with others, rather than constantly checking your phone.

Prioritize in-person activities and hobbies that don't involve technology (Shultz, 2021).

THE DANGERS OF CYBERBULLYING

One of the biggest dangers of digital communication is cyberbullying, which is the use of technology to harass, threaten, or humiliate someone. It's so important to take cyberbullying seriously because:

- Cyberbullying can have severe and long-lasting impacts on mental health, including increased risk of depression, anxiety, and suicidal thoughts.
- It can also lead to physical health problems, academic

difficulties, and substance abuse as victims struggle to cope with the emotional distress.

- The anonymity and accessibility of digital platforms can make it easier for bullies to target victims and harder for victims to escape the abuse.
- Being cyberbullied in a public forum like social media can amplify feelings of embarrassment, humiliation, or shame.

Research shows that cyberbullying is a significant problem among teenagers, particularly teenage boys. A 2019 study by the Pew Research Center found that 59% of U.S. teens have experienced some form of cyberbullying, with name-calling and rumor-spreading being the most common forms. The study also found that teenage boys were more likely than teenage girls to experience certain types of cyberbullying, such as physical threats and explicit images being shared without their consent (Anderson, 2018).

The impact of cyberbullying on teenage boys can be severe and long-lasting. A 2018 study published in the Journal of School Violence found that male adolescents who experienced cyberbullying were more likely to report symptoms of depression, anxiety, and suicidal thoughts compared to those who had not been cyberbullied. The study also found that the more frequent and severe the cyberbullying, the greater the impact on mental health (Bauman & Baldasare, 2018).

Another study published in the Journal of Youth and Adolescence in 2020 found that teenage boys who experienced cyberbullying were more likely to engage in substance abuse, aggression, and delinquent behavior compared to those who had not been cyberbullied. The researchers suggest that cyberbullying can lead to feelings of isolation, anger, and a desire for retaliation, which may manifest in harmful behaviors (Barlett et al., 2020).

If you or someone you know is experiencing cyberbullying, it's important to take action:

- Don't respond to the bully or engage with their behavior.

- Block the bully on social media and other communication platforms.
- Save evidence of the bullying, such as screenshots or messages.
- Tell a trusted adult, such as a parent, teacher, or counselor.
- Report the bullying to the social media platform or website where it's happening (National Bullying Prevention Center, 2022).

It's also important for parents, educators, and community members to be aware of the prevalence and impact of cyberbullying among teenage boys and to take proactive steps to prevent and address it. This may include:

- Educating students about digital citizenship and responsible online behavior.
- Implementing school policies and procedures for preventing and responding to cyberbullying.
- Providing support and resources for students who have experienced cyberbullying, such as counseling and peer support groups.
- Encouraging open communication and dialogue about cyberbullying and its impacts (U.S. Department of Health and Human Services, 2022).

REAL-LIFE STORY: OVERCOMING CYBERBULLYING

Ethan, a high school sophomore, shares his experience with cyberbullying and how he found support:

"When I was in 9th grade, I became the target of cyberbullying. A group of boys from my school created a fake social media account and used it to spread rumors about me and post embarrassing photos. I felt humiliated and alone.

At first, I was too embarrassed to tell anyone what was happening. But as the bullying escalated, I knew I needed help. I told my parents and my school counselor about the fake account and the bullying. They helped me report the account to the social media platform and document the bullying behavior.

My school also had an anti-bullying program that provided support and resources for students who were being bullied. I joined a support group with other students who had experienced cyberbullying, and we learned strategies for coping with the emotional impact and standing up to bullies.

It took time, but with the support of my family, friends, and school community, I was able to overcome the cyberbullying and rebuild my self-esteem. I learned that I didn't deserve to be treated that way and that there were people who had my back.

Now, I use my experience to help other students who are being bullied. I encourage them to speak up, seek help, and remember that they are not alone. Together, we can create a culture of kindness and respect, both online and off."

KEY TAKEAWAYS

- Digital communication can be a great way to stay connected, but it's important to maintain face-to-face interactions and build strong, in-person relationships.
- Cyberbullying is a serious issue that can have negative impacts on mental health and well-being.
- Too much screen time and technology use can lead to anxiety, depression, and other mental health challenges.
- To protect your mental health, limit your screen time, engage in offline activities, and seek support if needed.

By being mindful of how technology impacts your relationships and mental health, you can use it in a way that enhances your life and connections with others. Remember, technology is a tool, not a replacement for real-life interactions and experiences. Strive to find a healthy balance between online and offline activities, and don't hesitate to reach out for help if you're struggling with cyberbullying, addiction, or other technology-related challenges.

YOUR VOICE MATTERS: SHARE YOUR JOURNEY

"Your story is what you have, what you will always have. It is something to own." - Michelle Obama.

As you reach the halfway point of "Life Skills for Teenage Boys," take a moment to reflect on the transformative journey you've embarked upon. The insights, strategies, and real-life examples you've encountered so far have likely sparked new ideas, challenged old beliefs, and equipped you with the tools to navigate your teenage years with confidence.

Now, imagine the impact your story could have on another teenage boy who is struggling to find his way. Your unique experiences, challenges, and triumphs have the power to inspire, guide, and reassure him that he's not alone and that growth is possible.

By leaving an honest review of this book on Amazon, you're not just sharing your opinion—you're extending a lifeline to someone who may desperately need it. Your words can be the catalyst that empowers another teenage boy to take control of his life and unlock his full potential.

Here's how your review can make a difference:

Provide valuable insights and strategies that have worked for you, giving others a roadmap to success.

Offer encouragement and support, showing that challenges can be overcome with perseverance and the right tools.

Increase the book's visibility on Amazon, making it easier for more teenage boys to discover this life-changing resource.

To leave a review, simply click on this link or scan the QR code: https://www.amazon.com/review/review-your-purchases/?asin= B0D9ST7BHJ

Your voice matters, and your story has the power to change lives. Take a few moments to share your journey and help light the way for others.

Thank you for being an active participant in your own growth and for considering this opportunity to make a lasting impact on the lives of your peers.

Keep turning the pages—your next breakthrough awaits!

9

FINANCIAL LITERACY: BUILDING A STRONG FOUNDATION

"The most important investment you can make is in yourself"
— Warren Buffett.

Money management is one of the most critical skills you can develop as a teenager. Here's why building a strong financial foundation is so important:

- It helps you make informed decisions about earning, saving, and spending money, which can have a significant impact on your long-term financial well-being.
- It enables you to set and achieve financial goals, whether it's saving for a car, paying for college, or building an emergency fund.
- It teaches you to live within your means, avoid unnecessary debt, and make the most of your financial resources.
- It prepares you for the increasing financial responsibilities and challenges of adulthood, such as managing bills, taxes, and investments.
- It contributes to your overall sense of independence, security, and confidence in your ability to handle money matters.

BUDGETING BASICS

The first step to effective money management is creating a budget and having a budget is crucial because:

- It gives you a clear picture of your income and expenses, helping you understand where your money is going and where you may be able to cut back.
- It allows you to prioritize your spending based on your needs, wants, and goals, ensuring that you're allocating your money in a way that aligns with your values.
- It helps you avoid overspending, live within your means, and make the most of your financial resources.
- It enables you to track your progress toward your financial goals and make adjustments as needed.

To create a budget, start by tracking your spending for a few weeks to get a clear picture of where your money goes. Then, divide your expenses into categories, such as food, entertainment, and savings, and allocate a specific amount to each category based on your priorities and goals (Botting, 2019).

CHALLENGES AND SOLUTIONS

One of the biggest challenges in sticking to a budget is impulse spending. It's easy to get tempted by sales, trendy items, or social pressure to spend money on things you don't really need. To overcome this challenge, try the following strategies:

Wait 24-48 hours before making a non-essential purchase to see if you still want it.

Unsubscribe from retail emails and unfollow brands on social media to avoid temptation.

Set aside a small amount of "fun money" each month for discretionary spending.

Find free or low-cost alternatives for entertainment, such as hosting a movie night at home instead of going to the theatre.

REAL-LIFE STORY: HOW BUDGETING HELPED ME SAVE FOR MY FIRST CAR

Liam, a 16-year-old high school student, shares his experience with budgeting:

"When I got my first part-time job, I was excited to start earning my own money. However, I quickly realized that I was spending most of my paycheck on eating out and buying new video games. I knew I wanted to save up for a car, but at the rate I was going, it would take me forever.

That's when I decided to create a budget. I tracked my expenses for a month and was shocked to see how much I was spending on non-essentials. I set a goal to save $200 per month towards my car fund and cut back on eating out and gaming purchases.

It wasn't easy at first, but seeing my savings grow each month kept me motivated. After a year of sticking to my budget, I had saved enough for a down payment on a used car. The budgeting skills I learned have helped me manage my money more responsibly and work towards my long-term financial goals."

SAVING FOR THE FUTURE

Once you have a budget in place, it's essential to make saving a priority. Here's why saving money is so important, especially as a teenager:

- It helps you build a financial safety net for unexpected expenses or emergencies, giving you greater peace of mind and security.
- It allows you to take advantage of opportunities that may arise, such as traveling, pursuing a new hobby, or starting a business.

- It enables you to work towards larger financial goals, like paying for college, buying a house, or saving for retirement.
- It teaches you the value of delayed gratification and the importance of planning for the future.

Even if you can only save a small amount each month, those savings can add up over time, thanks to the power of compound interest. Make a habit of setting aside a portion of your income for savings, whether it's for a specific goal like a car or college or just for an emergency fund (Pritchard, 2021).

To make saving easier, consider automating your savings by setting up a direct deposit from your paycheck into a savings account. You can also use apps like Digit or Qapital, which analyze your spending patterns and automatically transfer small amounts of money into your savings based on what you can afford (Rosenberg, 2020).

EXPERT INSIGHT: THE IMPORTANCE OF STARTING EARLY

Henry Smith, a certified financial planner, emphasizes the power of starting to save early:

"The earlier you start saving, the more time your money has to grow through compound interest. For example, if you start saving $100 per month at age 15 and earn a 7% annual return, you'll have over $200,000 by age 60. If you wait until age 30 to start saving the same amount, you'll only have around $100,000 by age 60. That's the power of starting early."

UNDERSTANDING CREDIT AND DEBT

As you start to gain financial independence, it's crucial to understand how credit and debt work. Here's why it's important to use credit responsibly and avoid unnecessary debt:

- Building good credit can open up opportunities in the future, such as qualifying for a car loan, renting an apartment, or even getting a job.

- Using credit responsibly, such as paying your bills on time and keeping your balances low, demonstrates financial responsibility and can help you build a strong credit history.
- Taking on too much debt, especially high-interest debt like credit card balances, can be a major financial burden and limit your ability to save money or achieve your goals.
- Learning to live within your means and avoid unnecessary debt is an important part of maintaining financial stability and security.

Credit refers to the ability to borrow money with the promise to pay it back later, usually with interest. Building good credit is important for your financial future, as it can affect your ability to get loans, rent an apartment, or even get a job (Experian, 2019).

To build credit responsibly, consider getting a secured credit card or becoming an authorized user on a parent's card. Use the card for small purchases and make sure to pay off the balance in full each month to avoid accruing interest (Pascarella, 2021).

On the other hand, debt can be a major financial burden if not managed carefully. Avoid taking on unnecessary debt, such as high-interest credit card balances, and always have a plan for how you'll pay back any money you borrow (Fernando, 2021).

SELF-ASSESSMENT: ARE YOU READY FOR A CREDIT CARD?

Take this quiz to see if you're ready for the responsibility of a credit card:

1. Do you have a steady source of income?

a) Yes

b) No

2. Do you have a budget and track your spending?

a) Yes

b) No

3. Do you understand how credit card interest works?

a) Yes

b) No

4. Are you committed to paying off your balance in full each month?

a) Yes

b) No

If you answered "yes" to all four questions, you may be ready for a credit card. If you answered "no" to any of the questions, it's best to wait until you've developed stronger financial habits and knowledge.

LEARNING ABOUT INVESTING: A TEENAGE BOY'S GUIDE TO GROWING YOUR MONEY

Hey there, future Wall Street wizards! I know what you're thinking: "Investing? Isn't that something only old guys in suits do?" Well, guess what? You don't need a fancy degree or a corner office to start growing your money. In fact, the earlier you start, the more time your cash has to multiply. Investing means putting your money into assets like stocks, bonds, or mutual funds with the expectation that they will increase in value over time (Swart, 2022).

As a teenager, you have a huge advantage when it comes to investing: time. The earlier you start investing, the more time your money has to grow through the power of compound interest. Even small investments made now can have a significant impact on your financial future (Connick, 2021).

To get started with investing, consider opening a Roth IRA, which is a retirement account that allows you to invest money that has already been taxed. You can contribute up to $6,000 per year (as of 2022) and withdraw the money tax-free in retirement (Royal, 2021).

CASE STUDY: THE BENEFITS OF STARTING EARLY

Meet John and David. John started investing $100 a month in a Roth IRA at age 16, while David waited until he was 30 to start putting in $200 a month. Fast forward to age 60, and guess what? John has a whopping $470,000 in his account, while David only has around $300,000. That's the power of starting early and letting compound interest work.

TAXES AND YOUR PART-TIME JOB

If you have a part-time job, it's essential to understand how taxes work.

Understanding your tax obligations helps you avoid penalties or legal issues down the road.

Knowing how much of your income goes towards taxes can help you budget more accurately and plan for your financial goals.

Learning about taxes now prepares you for the increasing complexity of managing taxes as an adult, whether it's filing your own returns or working with a tax professional.

When you earn income, you're required to pay a portion of it to the government in the form of taxes. This includes federal income tax, as well as Social Security and Medicare taxes (H&R Block, 2022).

Your employer will typically withhold these taxes from your paycheck and send them to the government on your behalf. However, if you earn tips or work as an independent contractor (like babysitting or mowing lawns), you may be responsible for tracking your income and paying taxes on it yourself (TurboTax, 2021).

If you're unsure about your tax obligations, talk to a parent or consult a tax professional. They can help you navigate the tax system and ensure that you're following all the necessary rules and regulations.

INTERACTIVE ACTIVITY: CREATE YOUR OWN BUDGET

Now that you've learned the basics of budgeting, it's time to create your own budget. Follow these steps:

1. List your income sources and amounts.

2. List your expenses and categorize them (e.g., food, transportation, entertainment).

3. Set spending limits for each category based on your income and goals.

4. Use a budgeting app or spreadsheet to track your spending for the next month.

5. At the end of the month, review your spending and adjust your budget as needed.

Share your budget with a parent, mentor or friend and discuss your financial goals and challenges. Remember, budgeting is a skill that takes practice, so don't get discouraged if you don't get it perfect the first time.

KEY TAKEAWAYS

- Create a budget to track your income and expenses and allocate your money based on your priorities and goals.
- Make saving a priority, even if it's just a small amount each month, and consider automating your savings.
- Build credit responsibly by using credit cards wisely and avoiding unnecessary debt.
- Start investing early to take advantage of compound interest.

- Understand your tax obligations, especially if you have a part-time job.

By developing strong financial habits now, you'll be well-equipped to handle the financial challenges and opportunities that come with adulthood. Remember, it's never too early to start taking control of your financial future.

10

FINANCIAL PLANNING FOR COLLEGE AND BEYOND

"An investment in knowledge pays the best interest" —
Benjamin Franklin.

As you look ahead to your future education and career goals, it's important to start thinking about the financial aspects of these pursuits. College education, in particular, can be a significant investment. Here's why early financial planning is so crucial:

- It helps you make informed decisions about college choice, major, and career path based on a realistic understanding of costs and benefits.
- It enables you to access available resources, such as grants, scholarships, and work-study opportunities, to make college more affordable.
- It sets you up for long-term financial success by helping you develop budgeting, saving, and money management skills that will serve you well beyond college.
- It reduces financial stress and anxiety by giving you a clear plan and the tools to navigate the complex world of college finances.

- It empowers you to take control of your financial future and make choices that align with your goals and values.

UNDERSTANDING THE COSTS OF COLLEGE

The first step in financial planning for college is understanding the various costs associated with higher education. Having a clear picture of college expenses is important because:

It helps you create a realistic budget and savings plan based on your specific college goals and circumstances.

It allows you to compare the true costs of different colleges and make informed decisions about affordability and value.

It enables you to anticipate and prepare for hidden or indirect expenses, such as transportation, personal care, and social activities.

It empowers you to have informed conversations with family, advisors, and financial aid officers about your college plans and financing options.

These costs can include:

- Tuition and fees
- Room and board
- Textbooks and supplies
- Transportation
- Personal expenses

The specific costs will vary depending on factors like the type of institution (public vs. private), location, and program of study. Research the typical costs for colleges or programs you're interested in using tools like the College Board's Net Price Calculator or the U.S. Department of Education's College Scorecard.

It's also important to understand the difference between sticker price (the published cost of attendance) and net price (the actual cost after financial aid is applied). Many students pay less than the sticker price thanks to grants, scholarships, and other forms of financial assistance.

EXPLORING FINANCIAL AID OPTIONS

There are several types of financial aid available to help students and families pay for college:

Grants: Need-based financial aid that does not need to be repaid, such as the federal Pell Grant or state-specific grant programs.

Scholarships: Merit-based financial aid that does not need to be repaid, awarded based on factors like academic achievement, athletic ability, or community involvement. Scholarships can come from colleges, private organizations or community groups.

Work-study: A federal program that provides part-time jobs for undergraduate and graduate students with financial need, allowing them to earn money to help pay for education expenses.

Loans: Borrowed money that must be repaid with interest. Federal student loans, such as Direct Subsidized or Unsubsidized Loans, often have lower interest rates and more flexible repayment options compared to private loans.

To access most forms of financial aid, you'll need to complete the Free Application for Federal Student Aid (FAFSA). This form gathers information about your family's financial situation and helps determine your eligibility for federal, state, and institutional aid.

EXPERT INSIGHT: THE IMPORTANCE OF EARLY FAFSA FILING

Mark Kantrowitz, a leading expert on education finance and publisher of Savingforcollege.com, stresses the importance of filing the FAFSA as early as possible:

"Students who file the FAFSA in the first three months after it becomes available (October 1) tend to receive twice as much grant funding, on average,

compared to students who file the FAFSA later. This is because some finan-
cial aid programs have limited funds and distribute aid on a first-come, first-
served basis until the money runs out.

Even if you don't think you'll qualify for need-based aid, it's still worth filing
the FAFSA. Many colleges use the FAFSA to determine eligibility for merit-
based scholarships, and some private scholarships also require a completed
FAFSA. Plus, filing the FAFSA keeps your options open in case your finan-
cial circumstances change.

By making the FAFSA a priority and submitting it early, you can maximize
your chances of receiving the financial aid you need to make your college
dreams a reality."

RESEARCHING AND APPLYING FOR SCHOLARSHIPS

In addition to need-based financial aid, scholarships can be a valuable
way to fund your college education.

- Scholarships can provide free money for college that doesn't
  need to be repaid, reducing your overall cost and debt burden.
- Scholarships can be a way to be rewarded for your academic
  achievements, extracurricular activities, community
  involvement, or other talents and interests.
- The process of researching and applying for scholarships can
  help you clarify your goals, build important skills (like writing
  and self-advocacy), and make valuable connections in your
  field of interest.
- Winning scholarships can provide a sense of accomplishment
  and confidence, as well as help you stand out in future college
  and career applications.

Start researching scholarship opportunities early, using resources like:

- Your high school guidance office or college counseling center.
- Online scholarship search engines like Fastweb or
  Scholarships.com.

- Local community organizations, religious institutions, or service clubs.
- Professional associations or corporations related to your intended field of study.

Pay attention to scholarship deadlines and requirements and devote time and effort to crafting strong application essays and gathering necessary materials like transcripts and letters of recommendation.

REAL-LIFE EXAMPLE: MAXIMIZING SCHOLARSHIP OPPORTUNITIES

Jasmine, an 18-year-old high school senior, shares her experience with researching and applying for scholarships:

"As the first person in my family to attend college, I knew I would need to find ways to finance my education beyond just federal aid. I started researching scholarships in my junior year, using online search engines and talking to my school counselor.

I decided to focus my efforts on scholarships related to my intended major (computer science), my extracurricular activities (robotics club and volunteer tutoring), and my identity as a woman of color in STEM. I set aside time each week to work on scholarship applications, treating it like another class or part-time job.

Over time, my efforts paid off - I ended up receiving several scholarships, including a $10,000 award from a national organization supporting women in technology and a $5,000 scholarship from a local company. These funds, combined with grants and a part-time work-study job, allowed me to cover my college costs without taking on too much debt.

Looking back, I'm glad I made scholarship research and applications a priority. Not only did the money help make college more affordable, but the process also helped me clarify my goals, build my writing skills, and connect with supportive organizations in my field. I would encourage any student to start exploring scholarship opportunities early and to persist even if you face rejection along the way. Every little bit helps, and you never know what doors might open through the process."

BUDGETING AND FINANCIAL PLANNING STRATEGIES

As you prepare for college and beyond, it's important to develop strong budgeting and financial planning skills to manage your money effectively. Here are some strategies to consider:

Create a budget: Start by tracking your income and expenses for a few weeks to get a clear picture of where your money goes. Then, divide your expenses into categories, such as food, entertainment, and savings, and allocate a specific amount to each category based on your priorities and goals (Botting, 2019).

Differentiate between needs and wants: Prioritize essential expenses like tuition, housing, and food, and be mindful of discretionary spending on things like entertainment or dining out.

Look for ways to save money: Take advantage of student discounts, buy used textbooks, or explore alternative housing options like living at home or with roommates.

Consider part-time work: A part-time job or side hustle can help offset college costs and provide valuable work experience, as long as it doesn't interfere with your academic priorities.

Educate yourself about personal finance: Take advantage of resources like college financial literacy workshops, online courses, or books to learn about budgeting, saving, investing, and managing credit.

Plan for the long-term: While it may seem early, start thinking about your post-college financial goals, like paying off student loans, building an emergency fund, or saving for retirement. The earlier you start planning and saving, the more time you have to reach your goals.

INTERACTIVE ACTIVITY: COLLEGE COST COMPARISON

To make budgeting and saving easier, consider automating your savings by setting up a direct deposit from your paycheck into a savings account. You can also use apps like Digit or Qapital, which analyze your spending patterns and automatically transfer small amounts of money into your savings based on what you can afford (Rosenberg, 2020).

Remember, developing strong financial habits now will serve you well in college and beyond. By creating a budget, prioritizing your expenses, looking for ways to save money, and planning for the long term, you'll be better equipped to manage your finances and achieve your goals.

To get a hands-on understanding of college costs and budgeting, try this college cost comparison activity:

Choose three colleges or universities that interest you, making sure to include a mix of public and private institutions and in-state and out-of-state options.

Visit each school's website and research the following information:

- Tuition and fees
- Room and board
- Textbook and supply estimates
- Transportation costs
- Personal expenses

Create a spreadsheet to compare the costs for each school, broken down by category. Calculate the total cost of attendance for one year at each institution.

Research the average financial aid package for each school, including grants, scholarships, work-study, and loans. Subtract the average aid from the total cost of attendance to estimate the net price.

Reflect on the differences in costs and aid between the schools. Which option seems most affordable based on the net price? How might the costs influence your college decision-making process?

By engaging in this type of hands-on research and comparison, you can develop a more concrete understanding of college costs and start to build the budgeting and financial planning skills you'll need to manage your money in college and beyond.

SEEKING ADVICE AND SUPPORT

As you navigate the complex world of college finances, don't hesitate to seek advice and support from trusted sources. Here's why it's so important:

- Talking to people who have gone through the college financial planning process can provide valuable insights, tips, and lessons learned.
- Getting expert advice from financial aid officers, college counselors, or financial planners can help you understand your options and make informed decisions.
- Building a support network of family, friends, mentors, and organizations can provide encouragement, accountability, and resources as you work toward your college and career goals.
- Seeking help when you need it is a sign of strength and wisdom, not weakness – it shows that you are proactive, resourceful, and committed to your success.

Common trusted sources include:

- High school guidance counselors or college financial aid offices.
- Parents, guardians, or other family members with college experience.
- Mentors or professionals in your intended field of study.

- Non-profit organizations or community groups focused on college access and success.

Remember, you don't have to figure everything out on your own. Many people and resources are available to help you make informed financial decisions and access the support you need to achieve your college and career goals.

KEY TAKEAWAYS

- Understanding the costs of college, including tuition, room and board, textbooks, transportation, and personal expenses, is the first step in financial planning.
- Exploring financial aid options like grants, scholarships, work-study, and loans can help make college more affordable.
- Filing the FAFSA early can maximize your chances of receiving financial aid.
- Researching and applying for scholarships takes time and effort but can significantly reduce college costs.
- Developing budgeting and financial planning skills, like differentiating between needs and wants, looking for ways to save money, considering part-time work, and planning for the long term, is important for managing money in college and beyond.
- Seeking advice and support from trusted sources like counselors, family, mentors, and organizations can help you navigate the complex world of college finances.

11

CAREER EXPLORATION AND DEVELOPMENT

"The best way to predict the future is to create it." - Peter Drucker

As a teenage boy, you may be starting to think about your future career paths and goals. While you don't need to have your entire career mapped out, engaging in early career exploration and development is crucial for several reasons:

- It helps you identify your interests, strengths, and values, which can guide your educational and professional decisions.
- It allows you to make informed choices about high school courses, extracurricular activities, and post-secondary plans that align with your career goals.
- It provides opportunities to gain practical skills, experiences, and connections that can benefit you in future job searches or entrepreneurial ventures.
- It gives you a sense of direction and purpose, which can increase your motivation, engagement, and resilience in the face of challenges.

- It sets you up for long-term career satisfaction and success by helping you find a path that aligns with your passions and talents.

RESEARCHING POTENTIAL CAREER PATHS

One of the first steps in career exploration is researching potential career paths that align with your interests, skills, and values. This research is important because:

- It exposes you to a wide range of career options and possibilities, some of which you may not have considered or been aware of before.
- It provides valuable information about the day-to-day realities, challenges, and rewards of different jobs, helping you make more informed decisions.
- It helps you identify the education, skills, and experiences you'll need to pursue different career paths, allowing you to plan ahead and make strategic choices.
- It connects you with professionals and resources in your fields of interest, which can lead to mentorship, networking, and future opportunities.

Here are some strategies for investigating different career options:

Take career assessments: Many schools offer career assessments or inventories that can help you identify your strengths, interests, and potential career matches. These tools can provide a useful starting point for exploring different job families and industries.

Conduct informational interviews: Reach out to professionals in fields that interest you and request brief informational interviews to learn more about their career paths, day-to-day responsibilities, and advice for entering the field.

Attend career fairs and workshops: Participate in career fairs, workshops, or panels organized by your school, community organizations, or professional associations. These events provide opportunities to learn about different industries, network with professionals, and discover internship or job opportunities.

Explore online resources: Utilize online career exploration tools like O*NET OnLine, which provides detailed information on hundreds of occupations, including typical job duties, education requirements, and salary ranges. You can also follow industry blogs, podcasts, or social media accounts to stay up-to-date on trends and developments in fields of interest.

REAL-LIFE EXAMPLE: DISCOVERING A PASSION FOR ENVIRONMENTAL SCIENCE

Ethan, a 16-year-old high school student, shares how he explored his career interests and discovered a passion for environmental science:

"Growing up, I always enjoyed science classes and felt a strong connection to nature, but I wasn't sure how to translate those interests into a potential career path. In my sophomore year, I decided to start exploring my options more proactively.

First, I took a career assessment through my school's counseling office, which suggested several science-related career paths, including environmental science. This piqued my curiosity, so I started researching the field more online and through library resources.

I also reached out to a family friend who worked as an environmental engineer and requested an informational interview. She shared her educational background, career trajectory, and what she liked most about her work, which helped me understand the real-world applications of environmental science.

Finally, I attended a career fair focused on green jobs and sustainability, where I learned about different organizations and initiatives working to protect the environment. I left feeling inspired and excited about the possibility of contributing to this important work.

Through these experiences, I discovered a strong interest in environmental science and started to envision myself working in this field. I've since tailored my course selections and extracurricular activities to build relevant skills and knowledge, and I plan to pursue an environmental science degree in college.

While I'm still open to other possibilities, engaging in this early career exploration has given me a sense of direction and purpose as I navigate my high school years and prepare for my future."

GAINING RELEVANT EXPERIENCE

In addition to researching potential career paths, it's valuable to gain practical experience in fields of interest through internships, volunteer work, or part-time jobs. Here's why these experiences are so beneficial:

- They allow you to apply your knowledge and skills in real-world settings, giving you a taste of what it's really like to work in a particular field.
- They help you develop valuable professional skills, such as communication, teamwork, problem-solving, and leadership, which are transferable to any career.
- They provide opportunities to build your resume, portfolio, and professional network, which can give you a competitive edge in future job searches.
- They help you clarify your interests and goals by providing firsthand insight into what you like (or don't like) about different careers or work environments.

It's good to look for opportunities to get involved with organizations or projects related to your career interests, whether through school programs, community initiatives, or personal connections. Even if you start with small roles or responsibilities, you'll be gaining valuable exposure and experience that can benefit your future career.

EXPERT INSIGHT: THE VALUE OF NETWORKING

Dr. Ivan Misner, founder and chief visionary officer of Business Network International (BNI), emphasizes the importance of networking for career development:

"Networking is not just about exchanging business cards or connecting on LinkedIn - it's about building genuine, mutually beneficial relationships with others in your field or industry. These relationships can open doors to valuable opportunities, advice, and support throughout your career.

As a teenage boy, you may think that networking is something you don't need to worry about until you're actively job searching, but in reality, it's never too early to start building your professional network. Attend industry events, join school or community organizations related to your interests, and don't be afraid to reach out to professionals you admire for guidance or conversation.

Remember, networking is not about asking for favors or selling yourself - it's about creating authentic connections, learning from others' experiences, and finding ways to contribute value to your community. By starting to cultivate these relationships now, you'll be laying the foundation for a strong, supportive network that will serve you throughout your career journey."

PREPARING FOR FUTURE EDUCATION AND TRAINING

As you explore potential career paths, it's important to research the education and training requirements for jobs of interest. Different careers may require varying levels of education, from high school diplomas to advanced degrees, as well as specific certifications or licenses.

Use online resources like the Bureau of Labor Statistics' Occupational Outlook Handbook to investigate the typical education and training requirements for different occupations. This information can help you plan your high school course selections, extracurricular activities, and post-secondary education options to align with your career goals.

If you're considering pursuing higher education, start researching colleges, universities, or vocational programs that offer programs related to your fields of interest. Attend college fairs, visit campuses if possible, and connect with admissions counselors or faculty members to learn more about different programs and their requirements.

Remember, your career interests and goals may evolve over time, and that's okay. The key is to stay curious, proactive, and open to new opportunities and experiences that can help you grow and discover your unique path.

INTERACTIVE ACTIVITY: CAREER EXPLORATION SCAVENGER HUNT

To make career exploration more engaging and interactive, try this career scavenger hunt activity with a group of friends or classmates:

1. Compile a list of 10-15 career-related challenges or prompts, such as:

- Find a news article about an emerging trend or innovation in a field that interests you.
- Interview a professional in a career you're curious about and learn about their typical day-to-day responsibilities.
- Research the average salary and projected job growth for a specific occupation using the Bureau of Labor Statistics website.
- Attend a local career fair or industry event and collect business cards from three professionals you meet.
- Complete a free online course or tutorial related to a skill that's relevant to a potential career path.

2. Divide into teams or work individually to complete as many challenges as possible within a set time frame (e.g., one week or one month).

3. Reconvene as a group to share your findings, insights, and reflections. Discuss what you learned about different career paths, what surprised you, and what steps you might take to further explore your interests.

This activity encourages proactive, self-directed career exploration and helps make the process more social, competitive, and fun. By gamifying career research and skill-building, you and your friends can support and motivate each other while gaining valuable knowledge and experience.

DEVELOPING A HEALTHY RELATIONSHIP WITH CAREER PLANNING

As you engage in career exploration and planning, it's important to maintain a healthy, balanced perspective. Here's why:

- Your career is just one part of your multifaceted identity, and it's essential to cultivate other aspects of yourself, such as your relationships, hobbies, and personal growth.
- Putting too much pressure on yourself to have everything figured out can lead to stress, anxiety, and missed opportunities for exploration and self-discovery.
- In today's rapidly changing world, adaptability, flexibility, and resilience are key to career success, and these qualities are fostered by a growth mindset and openness to change.
- Your values, interests, and circumstances may shift over time, and it's important to give yourself permission to adjust your goals and plans accordingly.

Remember that your career is just one aspect of your life and identity, and it's okay if you don't have everything figured out right away. Some tips for maintaining a healthy mindset around career planning:

- Focus on exploring and learning, rather than putting pressure on yourself to make definitive decisions.

- Embrace trial and error - it's normal to change your mind or pivot your interests as you gain new experiences and insights.
- Prioritize your values, well-being, and relationships alongside your career aspirations.
- Seek support and guidance from mentors, teachers, or counselors when needed, but trust your own instincts and judgment.
- Celebrate your progress and accomplishments along the way, rather than fixating on end goals or outcomes.

By approaching career exploration with curiosity, openness, and self-compassion, you'll be better equipped to navigate the challenges and opportunities ahead and find a path that aligns with your unique talents, interests, and values.

KEY TAKEAWAYS

- Researching potential career paths involves taking assessments, conducting informational interviews, attending events, and exploring online resources.
- Gaining relevant experience through internships, volunteering, and part-time work can help build skills, explore interests, and make informed career decisions.
- Networking is an important skill for career development, and it's never too early to start building professional relationships.
- Understanding the education and training requirements for different careers can help guide high school course selection and post-secondary planning.
- Maintaining a healthy, balanced perspective on career planning involves focusing on exploration, embracing trial and error, prioritizing well-being, seeking support, and celebrating progress.

1 2

LEADERSHIP AND TEAMWORK SKILLS

"Teamwork makes the dream work, but a vision becomes a nightmare when the leader has a big dream and a bad team"
– John C. Maxwell.

As you navigate the challenges and opportunities of adolescence, developing strong leadership and teamwork skills is crucial for several reasons:

- It helps you build confidence, communication skills, and the ability to inspire and motivate others towards a common goal.
- It enables you to work effectively with diverse groups of people, fostering collaboration, respect, and shared success.
- It prepares you for future academic, professional, and personal roles where you'll need to take initiative, make decisions, and work as part of a team.
- It allows you to make a positive impact in your school, community, and beyond by mobilizing others to create meaningful change.
- It enhances your problem-solving, critical thinking, and adaptability skills, which are valuable in any context.

THE QUALITIES OF EFFECTIVE LEADERS

Effective leaders come in many different styles and personalities, but they often share some common qualities.

- Vision: Having a clear, compelling vision helps leaders set direction, inspire others, and maintain focus and motivation in the face of challenges.
- Integrity: Demonstrating honesty, ethical behavior, and consistency builds trust, credibility, and respect among team members and stakeholders.
- Empathy: Being able to understand and relate to others' perspectives and emotions allows leaders to build strong relationships, communicate effectively, and create an inclusive team environment.
- Communication: Clearly conveying ideas, expectations, and feedback, ensures that everyone is on the same page, motivated, and working towards the same goals.
- Adaptability: Being open to change, learning from mistakes, and adjusting strategies enables leaders to navigate complex, evolving situations and find creative solutions to problems (Doyle, 2022).

EXPERT INSIGHT: THE IMPORTANCE OF EMOTIONAL INTELLIGENCE IN LEADERSHIP

Dr. Michael Thompson, a leadership coach, highlights the role of emotional intelligence in effective leadership:

"Emotional intelligence is a crucial skill for effective leadership. Leaders who are self-aware, empathetic, and able to manage their own emotions are better equipped to build trust, resolve conflicts, and motivate their teams.

As a teenager, developing your emotional intelligence alongside your leadership skills can help you become a more effective and impactful leader. Practice active listening, perspective-taking, and regulating your own emotions in challenging situations. These skills will serve you well in any leadership role, whether in school, work, or your personal life."

STRATEGIES FOR DEVELOPING LEADERSHIP SKILLS

Developing leadership skills is an ongoing process that requires practice, reflection, and a willingness to step outside your comfort zone. Valuable strategies include:

Seek out leadership opportunities: Taking on leadership roles in various contexts allows you to practice and refine your skills, build your confidence, and demonstrate your potential to others.

Learn from role models: Observing and learning from effective leaders provides valuable insights, strategies, and inspiration that you can apply to your own leadership development.

Practice public speaking: Developing your communication skills helps you articulate your ideas, persuade and inspire others, and project confidence and credibility as a leader.

Take on new challenges: Pushing yourself to take on new responsibilities and projects stretches your abilities, builds your resilience, and expands your perspective and skill set.

Reflect on your experiences: Regularly reflecting on your leadership experiences allows you to identify your strengths, areas for improvement, and key lessons learned, enabling you to grow and adapt as a leader (Chekwa, 2018).

THE IMPORTANCE OF TEAMWORK

In addition to leadership skills, the ability to work effectively in a team is essential for success in many areas of life, including:

- Collaboration: Working cooperatively with others towards a common goal maximizes the team's collective talents, resources, and ideas, leading to better outcomes and shared success.

- Communication: Sharing ideas, actively listening to others, and providing constructive feedback fosters open dialogue, mutual understanding, and effective problem-solving within the team.
- Adaptability: Being open to new ideas, compromising when necessary, and adjusting to changing circumstances enables teams to remain agile, innovative, and resilient in the face of challenges.
- Responsibility: Following through on commitments, meeting deadlines, and being accountable for your work builds trust, reliability, and a sense of shared ownership within the team.
- Respect: Treating all team members with respect, regardless of their role or background, creates a positive, inclusive team culture that values diversity and encourages everyone to contribute their best (Doyle, 2021).

REAL-LIFE STORY: LEARNING TEAMWORK THROUGH ROBOTICS CLUB

Raj, a high school senior, shares his experience developing teamwork skills through his school's robotics club:

"When I joined my school's robotics club, I was excited to learn about programming and engineering. However, I quickly realized that building a successful robot required more than just technical skills - it required teamwork.

Our team had students with different strengths and backgrounds, from coding to design to project management. At first, we struggled to communicate effectively and work together towards our goals. We had disagreements over design choices and ran into delays due to miscommunication.

As the project progressed, we learned to play to each other's strengths and communicate more openly. We held regular team meetings to share updates, troubleshoot problems, and ensure everyone was on the same page. We also made an effort to listen to each other's ideas and perspectives, even when we disagreed.

Through this experience, I learned that effective teamwork requires clear communication, respect for each team member's contributions, and a willingness to adapt and compromise. I also learned that diversity of skills and perspectives can be a strength, as it allows the team to approach problems from multiple angles.

Now, as I prepare to graduate and head to college, I know that my teamwork skills will be key to my success. I'm confident that I have the tools and habits needed to work collaboratively, communicate effectively, and contribute to shared goals in any team setting."

THE BENEFITS OF DIVERSE TEAMS AND COMMUNITIES

In addition to developing leadership and teamwork skills, it's important to recognize the value of diversity in teams and communities. Diverse teams and communities bring together individuals with different backgrounds, perspectives, and experiences, leading to numerous benefits:

Enhanced creativity and innovation: Diverse teams can generate a wider range of ideas and solutions to problems. A study by McKinsey & Company found that companies in the top quartile for racial and ethnic diversity were 35% more likely to have financial returns above their respective national industry medians (Hunt et al., 2015).

Improved decision-making: Diverse teams can help mitigate biases and blind spots in decision-making. A study by Cloverpop found that inclusive teams made better business decisions up to 87% of the time (Larson, 2017).

Increased employee engagement and retention: Inclusive work environments where employees feel valued and respected, can lead to higher levels of engagement and lower turnover rates. A study by Deloitte found that organizations with inclusive cultures were six times more likely to be innovative and agile (Smith et al., 2020).

Enhanced student outcomes: Diverse schools and classrooms can provide students with valuable opportunities to learn from different perspectives and develop cross-cultural communication skills. A study by Wells et al. (2016) found that students who experienced greater diversity in school had higher levels of academic achievement, civic engagement, and awareness of inequality.

REAL-LIFE EXAMPLE: BUILDING AN INCLUSIVE COMMUNITY THROUGH A DIVERSITY CLUB

Samantha, a high school junior, shares her experience starting a diversity club at her school:

"I noticed that while our school was diverse, there wasn't much interaction between different groups of students. I wanted to create a space where students could come together, learn from each other's experiences, and build a more inclusive community.

I started a diversity club that met weekly to discuss topics related to identity, culture, and social justice. We invited guest speakers, held workshops, and organized events to celebrate our school's diversity. Through these activities, students from different backgrounds had the opportunity to share their stories, listen to other's perspectives, and develop empathy and understanding.

Over time, I noticed a positive change in our school's culture. Students were more open to interacting with peers from different groups, and there was a greater sense of belonging and respect. The diversity club also advocated for changes to make our school more inclusive, such as providing resources for English language learners and celebrating a wider range of cultural holidays.

Through this experience, I learned that diversity is not just about representation but about actively creating spaces for individuals to connect, learn, and grow together. By embracing diversity and building inclusive communities, we can tap into the strengths and insights of all individuals and create a more equitable and thriving society."

INTERACTIVE ACTIVITY: LEADERSHIP STYLE SELF-ASSESSMENT

Take this quiz to identify your dominant leadership style:

1. When making decisions, I typically:

a) Make decisions independently and expect others to follow my lead.

b) Seek input from team members, but make the final decision myself.

c) Facilitate group discussions and strive for consensus.

d) Delegate decision-making to team members with relevant expertise.

2. When motivating my team, I tend to:

a) Use rewards and consequences to incentivize performance.

b) Appeal to team members' sense of purpose and values.

c) Provide individual coaching and support to help each team member succeed.

d) Encourage team members to motivate and support each other.

3. When faced with a challenge or change, I usually:

a) Stick to the original plan and push through obstacles.

b) Adapt my approach based on feedback and changing circumstances.

c) Seek input from team members on how to adjust our strategy.

d) Encourage team members to develop and test new solutions.

4. My communication style can best be described as:

a) Direct and assertive, focusing on goals and expectations.

b) Supportive and empathetic, focusing on building relationships.

c) Collaborative and inclusive, focusing on gathering diverse perspectives.

d) Analytical and logical, focusing on facts and data.

If you answered mostly a's, your dominant leadership style may be Directive. If you answered mostly b's, your style may be Participative. Mostly c's suggests a Collaborative style, while mostly d's indicates a Delegative style.

Remember, there is no one "right" leadership style - effective leaders often adapt their approach based on the situation and the needs of their team. The key is to be self-aware, flexible, and responsive to feedback.

KEY TAKEAWAYS

- Effective leaders demonstrate vision, integrity, empathy, communication, and adaptability.
- Developing leadership skills requires practice, reflection, and a willingness to step outside your comfort zone.
- Teamwork involves collaboration, communication, adaptability, responsibility, and respect.
- Diverse teams and communities offer benefits such as enhanced creativity and innovation, improved decision-making, increased employee engagement and retention, and enhanced student outcomes.
- By developing strong leadership and teamwork skills and promoting diversity and inclusion, you can achieve your goals, make a positive impact, and prepare for success in your future career and relationships.
- Remember, leadership, teamwork, and diversity are essential for success in all areas of life. By seeking out opportunities to practice and develop these skills and actively promoting inclusivity, you can become a more effective leader, collaborator, and changemaker.

13

PUBLIC SPEAKING AND PRESENTATION SKILLS

"All the great speakers were bad speakers at first" - Ralph Waldo Emerson.

Public speaking and presentation skills are valuable assets for success in both academic and professional settings. Here's why developing these skills is crucial for teenage boys:

- It helps you communicate your ideas, knowledge, and opinions effectively, ensuring that your voice is heard and your perspectives are considered.
- It enhances your ability to persuade and influence others, which is essential for leadership, advocacy, and driving change.
- It boosts your confidence and self-assurance, helping you overcome fears and project a strong, capable presence.
- It prepares you for future academic and career challenges, such as presenting at conferences, pitching ideas to stakeholders, or delivering training sessions.
- It strengthens your critical thinking, storytelling, and

improvisational skills, which are valuable in many areas of life.

OVERCOMING PUBLIC SPEAKING ANXIETY

One of the biggest challenges in public speaking is overcoming fear and anxiety. It's important to manage these feelings because:

- Public speaking anxiety can hold you back from sharing your ideas, participating in class or meetings, or pursuing leadership opportunities.
- Nervousness can manifest in physical symptoms like shaking, sweating, or a quivering voice, which can distract from your message and undermine your credibility.
- Fear of public speaking can lead to avoidance, procrastination, or missed opportunities for growth and success.

It's common to feel nervous or intimidated when speaking in front of others, but there are strategies you can use to manage these feelings:

Practice deep breathing: Take slow, deep breaths from your diaphragm to calm your nerves and center yourself before and during your presentation.

Visualize success: Imagine yourself giving a confident, engaging presentation and receiving positive feedback from your audience. This mental rehearsal can help you feel more prepared and self-assured.

Focus on your message: Instead of worrying about your performance or the audience's reaction, focus on the content and value of your message. Reminding yourself of the importance of what you have to say can help you stay grounded and motivated.

Practice, practice, practice: The more you practice your presentation, the more comfortable and confident you'll feel. Practice in front of a mirror, record yourself, or ask friends or family members to be a mock audience.

Remember, it's okay to feel nervous - even experienced public speakers get butterflies sometimes. The key is to channel that energy into enthusiasm and passion for your topic.

EXPERT INSIGHT: THE POWER OF BODY LANGUAGE

Dr. Carol Kinsey Goman, an executive coach and author of "The Silent Language of Leaders," emphasizes the importance of nonverbal communication in public speaking:

"Your body language communicates just as much, if not more, than your words. To project confidence and engage your audience, stand up straight with your shoulders back and your feet shoulder-width apart. Make eye contact with individuals in the audience, smile genuinely, and use open, expressive gestures to reinforce your message.

Avoid closed-off or nervous body language like crossing your arms, fidgeting, or staring at your notes or slides. These nonverbal cues can make you appear unsure or disconnected from your audience.

By aligning your body language with your words and intentions, you can build trust, credibility, and rapport with your audience and deliver a more powerful, persuasive presentation."

PREPARING AND ORGANIZING YOUR PRESENTATION

Effective presentations start with thorough preparation and organization. Investing time in planning is so important because:

- Preparation helps you clarify your purpose, key messages, and desired outcomes, ensuring that your presentation is focused and impactful.
- Organizing your content into a logical structure makes it easier for your audience to follow your ideas and retain your main points.
- Designing engaging visuals supports your message, breaks up

text-heavy slides, and keeps your audience interested and attentive.
- Practicing your delivery allows you to refine your pacing, transitions, and overall flow, making your presentation more polished and professional.

Here are some steps to help you plan and structure your presentation:

Define your purpose and audience: Clearly identify the goal of your presentation and the needs, interests, and background of your audience. This will help you tailor your content and delivery to be most relevant and engaging.

Develop a clear, concise message: Distill your main points into a clear, concise message that your audience can easily understand and remember. Use evidence, examples, and stories to support your message and make it more compelling.

Create an outline: Organize your presentation into a logical, easy-to-follow structure with an introduction, main body, and conclusion. Use transitions to link your ideas and guide your audience through your argument.

Design engaging visuals: Use slides, images, charts, or other visual aids to reinforce your message and make your presentation more engaging. Avoid cluttering your visuals with too much text or data - keep them simple, clear, and visually appealing.

Practice and get feedback: Rehearse your presentation multiple times, ideally in front of an audience who can give you constructive feedback. Pay attention to your pacing, clarity, and engagement, and make adjustments as needed.

REAL-LIFE EXAMPLE: NAILING THE CLASS PRESENTATION

Marcus, a 17-year-old high school student, shares his experience preparing for and delivering a successful class presentation:

"In my English class, we were assigned to give a persuasive presentation on a topic of our choice. I decided to talk about the importance of mental health education in schools, a subject I'm passionate about.

To prepare, I started by researching the topic and gathering evidence to support my argument. I also thought carefully about my audience - my class-mates and teacher - and what would resonate most with them.

Next, I created an outline for my presentation, with an attention-grabbing introduction, three main points, and a strong conclusion. I designed a few simple slides with impactful images and statistics to reinforce my message.

I practiced my presentation several times, first alone and then in front of my family. I asked for their feedback on my content, delivery, and body language and made adjustments based on their suggestions.

On the day of the presentation, I was definitely nervous, but I used deep breathing and positive self-talk to stay calm and focused. During the presentation, I made eye contact with my classmates, used gestures to emphasize my points, and spoke with passion and conviction.

After I finished, I was thrilled to receive positive feedback from my teacher and classmates. They said my presentation was well-organized, persuasive, and engaging, and that I seemed confident and knowledgeable about the topic.

Through this experience, I learned that with thorough preparation, practice, and a genuine passion for your message, you can deliver a powerful presentation that inspires and informs your audience."

TIPS FOR ENGAGING YOUR AUDIENCE

One of the keys to a successful presentation is actively engaging your audience. Here are some strategies to help you capture and maintain your listeners' attention:

Start strong: Begin your presentation with a hook that grabs your audience's attention, such as a surprising statistic, a compelling story, or a thought-provoking question.

Make it interactive: Encourage audience participation by asking questions, soliciting feedback, or inviting volunteers to assist with demonstrations or examples.

Use humor and anecdotes: Incorporate appropriate humor, personal stories, or anecdotes to make your presentation more relatable and memorable.

Vary your tone and pace: Modulate your voice and vary your speaking pace to keep your audience engaged and emphasize key points.

Be authentic and passionate: Let your genuine enthusiasm and passion for your topic shine through in your delivery. Your energy and conviction can be contagious and inspire your audience to care about your message.

INTERACTIVE ACTIVITY: IMPROMPTU SPEAKING PRACTICE

To build your confidence and skills in public speaking, try this impromptu speaking activity:

1. Write down a variety of topics on slips of paper and place them in a bowl or hat. These can be fun, creative prompts like "If I were a superhero, my power would be..." or more serious topics like "The biggest challenge facing our generation is..."
2. Divide into pairs or small groups and take turns drawing a topic from the bowl.
3. Give each speaker 1-2 minutes to think about their topic, then have them deliver a short 2-3 minute impromptu speech on the subject.
4. After each speech, provide constructive feedback on the speaker's content, delivery, and engagement. Focus on praising strengths and offering specific, actionable suggestions for improvement.

5. Rotate through the group until everyone has had a chance to speak multiple times.

This activity helps you practice thinking on your feet, organizing your thoughts quickly, and delivering a clear, engaging message with minimal preparation. It also allows you to give and receive feedback in a supportive, low-stakes environment.

By developing your public speaking skills now, you'll be well-prepared to communicate effectively in a variety of academic and professional settings. Whether you're presenting a group project, pitching an idea, or delivering a keynote address, the strategies and techniques in this chapter will help you speak with confidence, clarity, and impact.

KEY TAKEAWAYS

- Overcoming public speaking anxiety involves techniques like deep breathing, visualization, focusing on your message, and practice.
- Effective body language, including good posture, eye contact, and open gestures, can enhance your credibility and connection with the audience.
- Preparing and organizing your presentation requires defining your purpose and audience, developing a clear message, creating an outline, designing engaging visuals, and practicing and seeking feedback.
- Engaging your audience involves strategies like starting strong, making it interactive, using humor and anecdotes, varying your tone and pace, and being authentic and passionate.
- Impromptu speaking practice can help build your confidence and skills in thinking on your feet and delivering clear messages with minimal preparation.

14

CONFLICT RESOLUTION AND NEGOTIATION SKILLS

"Peace is not the absence of conflict, but the ability to handle conflict by peaceful means" - Ronald Reagan.

As a teenager, you will inevitably face conflicts and disagreements with others, whether it's with friends, family members, classmates, or colleagues. Developing strong conflict resolution and negotiation skills is crucial for several reasons:

- It helps you maintain positive relationships with friends, family, classmates, and colleagues by effectively addressing disagreements and finding mutually beneficial solutions.
- It enhances your communication, empathy, and problem-solving abilities, which are essential for success in personal and professional settings.
- It reduces stress, anxiety, and negative emotions associated with unresolved conflicts or ongoing disputes.
- It prepares you for future challenges and opportunities that require the ability to navigate complex social dynamics, build consensus, and influence others.

- It contributes to a more harmonious, collaborative, and productive environment in your school, workplace, and community.

UNDERSTANDING CONFLICT

Conflict is a natural part of human interaction and can arise from differences in opinions, values, needs, or communication styles. Here's why it's important to view conflict as an opportunity for growth and learning:

- Conflict can expose underlying issues, misunderstandings, or inequities that need to be addressed for relationships and communities to thrive.
- Engaging in constructive conflict can lead to increased self-awareness, empathy, and perspective-taking as you learn to consider others' needs and viewpoints.
- Working through conflict can result in creative solutions, improved processes, and stronger, more resilient relationships built on a foundation of trust and respect.
- Developing the skills to handle conflict effectively can boost your confidence, resilience, and adaptability in the face of challenges and change.

While conflict can be uncomfortable or stressful, it can also be an opportunity for growth, learning, and positive change.

Some common sources of conflict include:

- Misunderstandings or miscommunications.
- Competing goals or priorities.
- Differences in values, beliefs, or perspectives.
- Limited resources or opportunities.
- Personality or style differences (Segal & Smith, 2020).

EXPERT INSIGHT: THE BENEFITS OF EFFECTIVE CONFLICT RESOLUTION

Dr. Jessica Nguyen, a conflict resolution expert, explains the positive outcomes of managing conflict constructively:

"Conflict is often seen as a negative experience, but when handled effectively, it can actually lead to positive outcomes. Effective conflict resolution involves finding a solution that meets the needs and interests of all parties involved rather than simply trying to win or avoid the conflict altogether.

Research has shown that individuals and teams that are able to manage conflict constructively tend to have higher levels of creativity, innovation, and job satisfaction. They are also more likely to build trust, respect, and collaboration in their relationships.

By developing your conflict resolution and negotiation skills as a teenager, you can set yourself up for success in your personal and professional life. You will be better equipped to handle difficult conversations, build stronger relationships, and find win-win solutions to challenges and opportunities."

THE FIVE CONFLICT RESOLUTION STYLES

According to the Thomas-Kilmann Conflict Mode Instrument, there are five main conflict resolution styles.

1. Competing: Pursuing your own interests at the expense of others.
2. Accommodating: Giving in to others' interests at your own expense.
3. Avoiding: Withdrawing from or delaying the conflict.
4. Collaborating: Working with others to find a mutually beneficial solution.
5. Compromising: Finding a middle ground that partially satisfies all parties (Kilmann Diagnostics, 2021).

Each style has its own strengths and weaknesses and may be more or less appropriate depending on the situation. For example, competing may be necessary in a crisis or emergency, while collaborating may be more effective for complex problems that require creative solutions.

The key is to be aware of your own default conflict resolution style and to develop the flexibility and skills to adapt your approach based on the needs and interests of the specific situation and parties involved.

STRATEGIES FOR EFFECTIVE CONFLICT RESOLUTION

Effective conflict resolution involves a combination of communication, problem-solving, and emotional intelligence skills, including:

Active listening: Giving your full attention and seeking to understand the other person's perspective demonstrates respect, builds trust, and helps you gather important information for finding a solution.

Expressing your needs and interests: Using "I" statements to clearly and assertively communicate your own perspective, feelings, and needs, without blaming or attacking, helps the other party understand your position and enables collaborative problem-solving.

Identifying common ground: Finding areas of agreement or shared interests, no matter how small, can provide a foundation for building consensus and generating mutually beneficial solutions.

Brainstorming options: Generating multiple potential solutions without judging or evaluating them at first encourages creative thinking, opens up new possibilities, and helps parties move beyond entrenched positions.

Evaluating and selecting a solution: Assessing the pros and cons of each option, based on objective criteria and the needs and interests of all parties, leads to a more balanced, sustainable resolution.

Implementing and following up: Putting the agreed-upon solution into action and checking it to ensure it's working as intended promotes accountability, follow-through, and ongoing communication to prevent future conflicts.

REAL-LIFE EXAMPLE: RESOLVING A GROUP PROJECT CONFLICT

Alistair, a high school senior, shares his experience resolving conflicts in a group project for his economics class:

"In my senior year of high school, I was assigned to a group project in my economics class. Our task was to create a business plan for a new product or service and present it to the class at the end of the semester.

At first, our group was excited about the project and had many creative ideas. However, as we started working on the details of the plan, we ran into some conflicts. Two members of the group had very different visions for the product and were constantly arguing and undermining each other's ideas. Another member was not pulling their weight and missing deadlines, which was frustrating for the rest of us.

As the project leader, I knew I needed to step in and help resolve these conflicts before they derailed our progress. I started by scheduling a group meeting to discuss the issues openly and honestly. I encouraged each member to express their perspective and needs, using "I" statements and active listening.

Through this conversation, we were able to identify the root causes of the conflicts. The two members with different visions realized that they actually had some common interests and were able to find a compromise that incorporated both of their ideas. The member who was not contributing agreed to take on a specific role and timeline for their tasks, with support and accountability from the rest of the group.

We also established some ground rules for communication and decision-making going forward, such as respecting each other's ideas, giving constructive feedback, and making decisions by consensus whenever possible.

As a result of these conflict resolution efforts, our group was able to work much more effectively and efficiently on our project. We ended up creating a strong business plan and delivering a successful presentation to the class.

Through this experience, I learned the importance of addressing conflicts early and directly rather than avoiding or ignoring them. I also learned the value of active listening, expressing needs and interests, and finding common ground in resolving disputes. These skills have served me well in other group projects, as well as in my personal relationships and job experiences.

Now, as I prepare to enter college and the workforce, I feel more confident in my ability to handle conflicts and negotiate solutions. I know that these skills will be essential for success in any field or industry, and I am committed to continuing to develop and apply them throughout my life."

INTERACTIVE ACTIVITY: CONFLICT RESOLUTION ROLE-PLAY

To practice your conflict resolution and negotiation skills, try this role-play activity with a partner:

Choose a conflict scenario, such as:

- Two friends disagree over how to spend their weekend.
- A student and teacher have different expectations for a project.
- Siblings argue over household chores and responsibilities.

Assign roles to each person, and take a few minutes to prepare your character's perspective, needs, and interests.

Role-play the conflict scenario, using the strategies for effective conflict resolution (active listening, expressing needs and interests, identifying common ground, etc.).

After the role-play, debrief with your partner: What strategies did you use? What worked well and what didn't? What did you learn about conflict resolution and negotiation?

By practicing conflict resolution and negotiation skills in a safe and structured environment, you can develop your confidence and competence in handling real-life conflicts and disputes.

NEGOTIATION SKILLS

Negotiation is a specific type of conflict resolution that involves finding an agreement or compromise between two or more parties with different needs, interests, or positions. Here's why developing effective negotiation skills is important:

- Negotiation is a key aspect of decision-making, problem-solving, and relationship-building in personal and professional contexts.
- Effective negotiation can help you achieve your goals while also taking into account the needs and interests of others involved.
- Negotiation skills enable you to influence others, build alliances, and create value in situations where resources or options may be limited.
- Developing a collaborative, problem-solving approach to negotiation can lead to more creative, mutually beneficial outcomes and stronger, more positive relationships.

Some key negotiation skills include:

Preparation: Research the issue, the other party's perspective and interests, and your own goals and priorities before the negotiation.

Communication: Use active listening, ask questions, and express your needs and interests clearly and respectfully.

Emotional intelligence: Manage your own emotions and reactions, and be attuned to the other party's feelings and nonverbal cues.

Creativity: Think outside the box and generate multiple options or proposals that could meet both parties' needs.

Flexibility: Be open to alternative solutions and willing to make trade-offs or concessions to reach an agreement.

Persistence: Stay focused on your goals and interests, and don't give up easily in the face of obstacles or resistance (Harvard Law School, 2021).

By developing and applying these negotiation skills, you can become a more effective and successful communicator, problem-solver, and leader in all areas of your life.

KEY TAKEAWAYS

- Conflict is a natural part of human interaction, and can be an opportunity for growth, learning, and positive change when handled effectively.
- There are five main styles of conflict resolution: competing, accommodating, avoiding, collaborating, and compromising.
- Effective conflict resolution involves active listening, expressing needs and interests, identifying common ground, brainstorming options, and selecting and implementing a solution.
- Negotiation is a specific type of conflict resolution that involves finding an agreement or compromise between two or more parties with different needs, interests, or positions.
- Key negotiation skills include preparation, communication, emotional intelligence, creativity, flexibility, and persistence.

Remember, conflict resolution and negotiation are skills that can be developed and improved over time. By practicing these skills in your daily life and relationships, you can become a more effective communicator, problem-solver, and leader and build stronger, more positive connections with others.

15

CREATIVITY AND INNOVATION

"Creativity is intelligence having fun" - Albert Einstein.

As a teenager, you have a unique opportunity to tap into your creativity and imagination to develop innovative solutions to the challenges facing yourself, your community, and the world. Cultivating creativity and innovation skills is crucial for several reasons:

- It enables you to think outside the box and develop unique solutions to problems, giving you a competitive edge in school, work, and life.
- It allows you to express your individuality, passions, and talents in meaningful ways, contributing to a sense of purpose and fulfillment.
- It prepares you for success in a rapidly changing world, where the ability to adapt, innovate, and create value is increasingly important.
- It enhances your ability to collaborate with diverse people, perspectives, and disciplines, leading to more robust and impactful outcomes.

- It provides a healthy outlet for exploring your interests, taking risks, and learning from failures, fostering resilience and personal growth.

THE IMPORTANCE OF CREATIVITY

Creativity is the ability to generate new and original ideas, solutions, or expressions.

In today's complex and dynamic world, the ability to think creatively and generate innovative solutions is essential for tackling global challenges and driving progress.

Creativity allows individuals and organizations to differentiate themselves, create value, and compete in crowded markets or industries.

Engaging in creative activities and pursuits can provide a sense of joy, fulfillment, and self-expression, contributing to overall well-being and life satisfaction.

Developing creativity skills can transfer to other areas of life, enhancing problem-solving, communication, and adaptability in personal and professional contexts.

It is a critical skill for success in the 21st century, as it enables individuals and organizations to adapt to change, solve complex problems, and drive innovation in all areas of life.

Benefits of creativity include:

- Improved problem-solving and decision-making skills.
- Enhanced self-expression and communication.
- Increased resilience and adaptability in the face of challenges.
- Greater job satisfaction and career success.
- Positive impact on mental health and well-being (Adobe, 2016).

EXPERT INSIGHT: THE CREATIVE PROCESS

Dr. Emily Chen, a creativity and innovation researcher, explains the creative process and how to develop creativity skills:

"Creativity is not just a talent that some people are born with - it is a skill that can be developed and strengthened over time. The creative process typically involves four stages: preparation, incubation, illumination, and verification.

In the preparation stage, you gather information, resources, and inspiration related to the problem or challenge you want to address. In the incubation stage, you let your mind wander and make connections between different ideas and concepts. In the illumination stage, you have a sudden insight or "aha" moment where a new idea or solution emerges. And in the verification stage, you test and refine your idea to ensure it is viable and effective.

By understanding and practicing each stage of the creative process, you can develop your creativity skills and unlock your potential for innovation and impact."

STRATEGIES FOR CULTIVATING CREATIVITY

Cultivating creativity is an ongoing process that requires curiosity, openness, and a willingness to take risks and learn from failure.

Engage in diverse experiences: Exposing yourself to new and varied ideas, perspectives, and domains helps spark novel connections and insights, fueling creative thinking.

Practice brainstorming: Generating multiple ideas without judgment helps overcome mental blocks, encourages divergent thinking, and leads to more innovative solutions.

Embrace mistakes and failures: Reframing setbacks as opportunities for learning and growth fosters a growth mindset, resilience, and a willingness to take creative risks.

Collaborate with others: Working with people from different backgrounds and areas of expertise brings diverse knowledge and perspectives, leading to more robust and creative outcomes.

Take breaks and rest: Allowing your mind to recharge and wander freely can activate the default mode network, enabling unconscious processing and "Eureka!" moments of creative insight (Gregoire, 2018).

THE POWER OF INNOVATION

Innovation is the process of creating new and improved products, services, or processes that solve real-world problems and meet the needs of individuals, organizations, or society. Innovation is so powerful because:

- Innovation drives economic growth, creates jobs, and improves living standards by introducing new and better ways of doing things.
- It enables individuals and organizations to stay relevant, competitive, and impactful in the face of changing customer needs, technological advancements, and societal challenges.
- Innovative solutions can tackle complex global issues, such as climate change, healthcare access, or educational inequity, improving the lives of millions.
- Engaging in innovation fosters a culture of continuous learning, experimentation, and improvement, leading to more agile and adaptable individuals and organizations.

It involves identifying challenges, generating novel ideas, and implementing solutions that create tangible value and positive change.

Examples of innovation in various fields include:

Technology: The development of smartphones has revolutionized communication, providing people with access to information, services, and social connections at their fingertips. For instance, the iPhone, first introduced by Apple in 2007, combined a phone, music player, and internet browser into one portable device, setting a new standard for mobile technology (Nguyen, 2018).

Medicine: The discovery of penicillin by Alexander Fleming in 1928 revolutionized the treatment of bacterial infections, saving countless lives and paving the way for the development of other antibiotics. Today, researchers continue to innovate in medicine, developing new vaccines, therapies, and diagnostic tools to combat diseases and improve patient outcomes (Tan & Tatsumura, 2015).

Education: The Khan Academy, founded by Salman Khan in 2008, has transformed the way students learn by providing free, high-quality educational content online. With over 100 million registered users and thousands of video lessons, the platform has made education more accessible and personalized, particularly for students in underserved communities (Khan Academy, 2021).

Business: The sharing economy, exemplified by companies like Airbnb and Uber, has disrupted traditional business models by leveraging technology to connect consumers with underutilized resources, such as apartments and cars. These innovative platforms have created new economic opportunities, increased efficiency, and provided consumers with more convenient and affordable options (Sundararajan, 2016).

Social impact: The micro-lending platform Kiva, founded in 2005, has pioneered a new approach to alleviating poverty by enabling individuals to lend small amounts of money to entrepreneurs in developing countries. By providing access to capital and empowering borrowers to start or grow their businesses, Kiva has helped over 4 million people in 77 countries improve their livelihoods and communities (Kiva, 2021).

REAL-LIFE EXAMPLE: INVENTING A SOLUTION TO FOOD WASTE

These examples demonstrate how innovation can lead to concrete, measurable impacts across various domains, from improving individual lives to transforming entire industries and societies. By identifying pressing needs, challenging assumptions, and developing creative solutions, innovators have the power to drive meaningful progress and shape a better future for all.

Jasmine, a high school senior, shares her experience using creativity and innovation to develop a mobile app that reduces food waste and supports food banks:

"When I volunteered at my local food bank, I was shocked to learn about the amount of food that goes to waste in our community. I saw firsthand how many people were struggling with food insecurity while perfectly good food was being thrown away by restaurants, grocery stores, and households.

I decided to use my passion for technology and my creativity skills to develop a solution. I came up with the idea for a mobile app that would connect surplus food from local businesses with food banks and shelters in real time.

I started by researching the problem of food waste and the existing solutions in the market. I also reached out to local food banks and businesses to understand their needs and challenges. Then, I began brainstorming and prototyping different features and designs for the app.

It was a challenging process, as I had to learn new coding skills, navigate legal and logistical issues, and pitch my idea to potential partners and investors. I faced many setbacks and failures along the way, but I used them as opportunities to learn and improve my app.

After months of hard work and collaboration with my team, we launched our app in the community. It was amazing to see the impact it had on reducing food waste and supporting those in need. Restaurants and grocery stores could easily donate their surplus food, and food banks and shelters could quickly receive and distribute the donations to their clients.

Through this experience, I learned that creativity and innovation have the power to solve real-world problems and make a positive difference in people's lives. I also learned the importance of perseverance, collaboration, and learning from failure in the creative process.

Now, as I graduate and pursue my career in technology, I plan to continue using my creativity skills to develop innovative solutions to the challenges facing our world. Whether it's in the fields of sustainability, healthcare, education, or social impact, I know that every idea counts in creating a better future for all."

INTERACTIVE ACTIVITY: THE MARSHMALLOW CHALLENGE

To practice your creativity and innovation skills, try the Marshmallow Challenge with a group of friends or classmates:

1. Divide into teams of 3-5 people.
2. Each team receives 20 sticks of spaghetti, one yard of tape, one yard of string, and one marshmallow.
3. The goal is to build the tallest freestanding structure with the marshmallow on top, using only the materials provided.
4. Teams have 18 minutes to complete the challenge.
5. After the challenge, reflect on the creative process: What strategies did your team use? What worked well and what didn't? What did you learn about collaboration, risk-taking, and learning from failure?

The Marshmallow Challenge is a fun and engaging way to practice creative problem-solving, teamwork, and innovation skills. It also demonstrates the importance of prototyping, testing, and iterating in the creative process.

- Creativity is a critical skill for success in the 21st century, as it enables individuals and organizations to adapt to change, solve complex problems, and drive innovation.
- The creative process involves four stages: preparation, incubation, illumination, and verification.
- Cultivating creativity requires curiosity, openness, and a willingness to take risks and learn from failure.
- Innovation is the process of creating new and improved products, services, or processes that add value and meet the needs of individuals, organizations, or society.
- Developing creativity and innovation skills can help you unlock your potential as a changemaker and pioneer in your chosen field.

Remember, creativity and innovation are skills that can be developed and strengthened over time. By engaging in diverse experiences, practicing brainstorming and problem-solving, embracing mistakes and failures, collaborating with others, and taking breaks and rest, you can cultivate your creativity and unlock your potential for impact and success.

16

CULTURAL COMPETENCE AND
DIVERSITY AWARENESS

"No one is born hating another person because of the color of his skin, or his background, or his religion. People must learn to hate, and if they can learn to hate, they can be taught to love, for love comes more naturally to the human heart than its opposite" - Nelson Mandela.

In today's increasingly diverse and interconnected world, developing cultural competence and awareness of diversity is essential for teenage boys for several reasons:

- It prepares you to live, work, and thrive in a multicultural society, where you will interact with people from diverse backgrounds in various settings.
- It enables you to build strong, respectful relationships with people who may have different identities, experiences, and perspectives from your own.
- It enhances your ability to communicate effectively, collaborate, and navigate cross-cultural challenges in personal, academic, and professional contexts.

- It fosters empathy, open-mindedness, and critical thinking skills that are essential for personal growth, social responsibility, and global citizenship.
- It equips you to be an advocate and ally for social justice, working to create more inclusive and equitable communities for all.

UNDERSTANDING THE DIMENSIONS OF DIVERSITY

Diversity encompasses a wide range of human differences, including but not limited to:

- Race and ethnicity.
- Gender identity and expression.
- Sexual orientation.
- Age.
- Physical and mental ability.
- Religion and spirituality.
- Socioeconomic status.
- Language and nationality.
- Political beliefs and affiliations.

Each of these dimensions of diversity intersects and influences an individual's experiences, perspectives, and opportunities in unique ways. Developing an understanding of these diverse identities and experiences is a key component of cultural competence.

REAL-LIFE EXAMPLE: LEARNING FROM DIVERSE PERSPECTIVES

Daniel, a 17-year-old high school student, shares his experience with cultural competence and diversity awareness:

"Growing up in a predominantly white, middle-class neighborhood, I had limited exposure to diversity in my early years. It wasn't until I started high

school and joined the debate team that I began to really engage with people from different backgrounds and perspectives.

Through debate, I had the opportunity to research and discuss complex social and political issues with teammates and competitors from all walks of life. I learned to listen actively, ask questions respectfully, and consider viewpoints that were different from my own.

One experience that particularly stands out was when I was paired with a teammate who was a recent immigrant from Honduras for a debate on immigration policy. As we prepared our arguments, she shared her personal story of coming to the United States and the challenges her family faced in the process. Her experiences put a human face on an issue that I had previously only understood in abstract terms.

Through this collaboration, I gained a deeper appreciation for the complexity of immigration and the importance of considering the real-life impacts of policy decisions on diverse communities. I also learned valuable lessons about the power of empathy, perspective-taking, and respectful dialogue in bridging cultural divides.

Since then, I've made a conscious effort to seek out opportunities to engage with people from diverse backgrounds, whether through volunteer work, cultural events, or simply striking up conversations with classmates or neighbors I might not have interacted with otherwise. I've learned that we can find common ground and build stronger, more inclusive communities by approaching differences with curiosity, humility, and an open mind."

STRATEGIES FOR DEVELOPING CULTURAL COMPETENCE

Developing cultural competence is an ongoing, lifelong process that requires self-reflection, education, and a willingness to step outside one's comfort zone.

Examine your own biases and assumptions: Recognizing and challenging your own implicit biases is crucial for developing self-awareness, empathy, and the ability to build authentic relationships across differences.

Educate yourself about different cultures and identities: Actively seeking out diverse perspectives and experiences helps broaden your understanding, challenge stereotypes, and develop a more nuanced and respectful approach to cultural differences.

Engage in diverse experiences and relationships: Immersing yourself in diverse communities and building relationships based on mutual learning and respect fosters empathy, trust, and the ability to navigate cross-cultural challenges effectively.

Practice active listening and perspective-taking: Developing the skills to listen deeply, ask questions respectfully, and see situations from multiple viewpoints enhances your ability to communicate, collaborate, and build bridges across differences.

Advocate for inclusion and equity: Using your privilege and influence to challenge systemic inequities and create more inclusive environments demonstrates your commitment to social justice and helps create a more equitable world for all.

INTERACTIVE ACTIVITY: CULTURAL COMPETENCE SELF-ASSESSMENT

To gauge your current level of cultural competence and identify areas for growth, try this self-assessment activity:

Reflect on your own cultural background and identity. How have your experiences and upbringing shaped your attitudes, beliefs, and behaviors related to diversity?

Consider your current knowledge and understanding of different cultures and identities. On a scale of 1-5, how would you rate your familiarity with the experiences, perspectives, and challenges faced by diverse groups, such as:

- Racial and ethnic minorities.
- LGBTQ+ individuals.
- People with disabilities.

- Religious minorities.
- Immigrants and refugees.

Assess your level of engagement with diverse communities and perspectives. On a scale of 1-5, how often do you:

- Interact with people from different backgrounds in meaningful ways.
- Seek out information and resources about diverse cultures and identities.
- Participate in events or initiatives that promote diversity and inclusion.
- Speak out against discrimination and prejudice when you encounter it.

Identify areas where you would like to grow in your cultural competence. What specific knowledge, skills, or experiences do you need to develop to become a more effective ally and advocate for diversity and inclusion?

Create an action plan for enhancing your cultural competence. Set specific, measurable goals for learning about different cultures, engaging in diverse experiences, and promoting equity and inclusion in your spheres of influence.

By regularly assessing your own cultural competence and taking proactive steps to grow in your understanding and advocacy, you can become a more effective leader and change agent in creating a more just and inclusive society.

THE BENEFITS OF DIVERSE TEAMS AND COMMUNITIES

Research has shown that diversity and inclusion are not only moral imperatives but also have tangible benefits for individuals, organizations, and society as a whole. Diverse teams and communities are so valuable for the following reasons:

Enhanced creativity and innovation: Diverse teams bring a wider range of perspectives, experiences, and ideas to problem-solving and decision-making, leading to more creative and innovative solutions (Hunt et al., 2018).

Improved academic and career outcomes: Students who interact with diverse peers and engage in cross-cultural learning experiences tend to have better academic performance, critical thinking skills, and preparation for future careers (Wells et al., 2016).

Stronger social and emotional skills: Exposure to diversity helps individuals develop empathy, perspective-taking, and cross-cultural communication skills, which are essential for building strong relationships and navigating an increasingly diverse world (Bowman, 2011).

More equitable and inclusive environments: When diversity and inclusion are prioritized, organizations and communities can create more welcoming and supportive environments for people of all backgrounds, leading to better outcomes and a greater sense of belonging for all (Shore et al., 2018).

EXPERT INSIGHT: THE IMPORTANCE OF DIVERSITY IN EDUCATION

Dr. Beverly Daniel Tatum, a renowned psychologist and author of "Why Are All the Black Kids Sitting Together in the Cafeteria? And Other Conversations About Race," emphasizes the importance of diversity in education:

"When we don't talk about race and racism with young people, we leave them to draw their own conclusions about the social world around them. Often, those conclusions are based on limited information and biased by stereotypes and misinformation.

Schools have a critical role to play in helping students develop the knowledge, skills, and attitudes needed to function effectively in a diverse society. By providing opportunities for students to learn about and engage with people from different backgrounds, schools can help break down stereotypes, promote cross-cultural understanding, and prepare students to be active, informed citizens in a multicultural world.

However, it's not enough to simply have diversity present in a school or classroom. Educators must also create inclusive environments where all students feel valued, respected, and supported in their learning and development. This requires a commitment to ongoing professional development, curricular reform, and community engagement to ensure that diversity and equity are woven into the fabric of the educational experience."

ADVOCATING FOR DIVERSITY AND INCLUSION

As a teenage boy, you have the power to be an advocate and ally for diversity and inclusion in your school, community, and future workplaces. Some ways to get involved and make a difference include:

Educate yourself and others: Continue learning about diverse cultures, identities, and social issues, and share your knowledge with others through conversations, social media, or advocacy campaigns.

Challenge stereotypes and prejudice: Speak out against biased language, jokes, or behaviors when you encounter them, and encourage others to do the same. Use your privilege to amplify the voices and experiences of marginalized groups.

Support diversity and inclusion initiatives: Get involved with clubs, organizations, or events that promote diversity and inclusion in your school or community, such as multicultural student associations, diversity conferences, or community dialogues.

Advocate for systemic change: Use your voice and platform to advocate for policies, practices, and resources that support diversity, equity, and inclusion, such as diverse curriculum, bias training for educators, or increased funding for community-based organizations.

Build authentic relationships: Seek out opportunities to connect with people from different backgrounds in genuine, respectful ways.

Listen to their stories, learn from their experiences, and work together to create more inclusive and equitable communities.

Remember, advocating for diversity and inclusion is a lifelong journey that requires ongoing learning, reflection, and action. By committing to this work as a teenage boy, you can help create a more just and equitable world for yourself and future generations.

KEY TAKEAWAYS

- Diversity encompasses a wide range of human differences, including race, ethnicity, gender identity, sexual orientation, ability, religion, socioeconomic status, and more.
- Developing cultural competence involves examining your own biases, educating yourself about different cultures, engaging in diverse experiences, practicing active listening and perspective-taking, and advocating for inclusion and equity.
- Diverse teams and communities offer benefits like enhanced creativity, improved academic and career outcomes, stronger social-emotional skills, and more equitable environments.
- Educators play a key role in creating inclusive learning environments that help students develop the skills to thrive in a diverse society.
- Teenage boys can be powerful advocates for diversity and inclusion by educating themselves and others, challenging bias, supporting initiatives, advocating for change, and building authentic relationships.

17

ENVIRONMENTAL RESPONSIBILITY AND SUSTAINABILITY

"The greatest threat to our planet is the belief that someone else will save it" - Robert Swan.

As a teenager, you have the power to make a positive impact on the environment and promote sustainability for future generations. Taking responsibility for the environment and promoting sustainability is crucial for several reasons:

- Your generation will face the most severe consequences of environmental degradation, such as climate change, pollution, and resource depletion, making it essential to take action now.
- You have the power to influence your peers, family, and community by modeling sustainable behaviors and advocating for eco-friendly practices.
- Developing a sense of environmental stewardship and responsibility prepares you to be a conscientious, ethical leader in your future personal and professional life.
- Contributing to a healthier, more sustainable world benefits not only the planet but also your own physical and mental well-being, as well as that of future generations.

- As a global citizen, you have a moral obligation to protect and preserve the Earth's natural resources and ecosystems for all living beings.

UNDERSTANDING ENVIRONMENTAL ISSUES

The first step in promoting environmental responsibility is to educate yourself about the key issues facing our planet.

Awareness of environmental challenges enables you to make informed decisions about your own behaviors and consumption patterns and to advocate for sustainable policies and practices.

Understanding the science behind issues like climate change and biodiversity loss equips you to communicate effectively with others and counter misinformation or denial.

Recognizing the interconnectedness of environmental issues with social and economic justice helps you develop a holistic, systems-thinking approach to sustainability.

Knowledge of the urgency and scale of environmental problems can motivate you to take action and inspire others to join the cause.

Some of the most pressing environmental challenges include:

Climate change: The warming of the Earth's atmosphere due to human activities such as burning fossil fuels and deforestation.

Biodiversity loss: The extinction of plant and animal species due to habitat destruction, pollution, and other human impacts.

Pollution: The contamination of air, water, and soil with harmful substances such as chemicals, plastic, and waste.

Resource depletion: The overuse and mismanagement of natural resources such as water, forests, and minerals (National Geographic Society, 2022).

EXPERT INSIGHT: THE IMPORTANCE OF YOUTH ENGAGEMENT

Dr. Sarah Thompson, an environmental scientist and educator, emphasizes the importance of youth engagement in addressing environmental challenges:

"Young people have a critical role to play in addressing environmental challenges and promoting sustainability. As the generation that will inherit the planet, you have the most at stake in ensuring a healthy, thriving world for yourselves and future generations.

Research has shown that youth engagement in environmental issues can lead to significant positive impacts, from reducing household energy use and waste to influencing policy decisions and corporate practices. By educating yourself about environmental challenges, adopting sustainable habits, and advocating for change, you can help create a more just and sustainable world for all."

ADOPTING SUSTAINABLE HABITS

One of the most powerful ways to promote environmental responsibility is to adopt sustainable habits in your own life. Here's why your individual actions matter:

- Personal behavior change, when adopted by many people, can add up to significant environmental impact, such as reducing greenhouse gas emissions or conserving natural resources.
- Modeling sustainable habits can influence your family, friends, and community to adopt similar practices, creating a ripple effect of positive change.
- Developing eco-friendly habits early in life sets you up for a lifetime of environmental responsibility and can inspire future generations to follow in your footsteps.
- Aligning your daily actions with your values of sustainability fosters integrity, accountability, and a sense of empowerment to make a difference.

Some eco-friendly practices you can start today include:

Reduce, reuse, recycle: Minimize your waste by reducing your consumption of single-use products, reusing items when possible, and recycling materials like paper, plastic, and glass.

Conserve energy: Turn off lights and electronics when not in use, use energy-efficient appliances, and opt for renewable energy sources like solar or wind power when possible.

Save water: Take shorter showers, fix leaky faucets, and choose drought-tolerant plants for your garden.

Eat sustainably: Choose plant-based meals, buy local and organic produce, and reduce your food waste by composting or donating excess food.

Travel green: Walk, bike, or use public transportation instead of driving, and consider eco-friendly options like electric or hybrid vehicles (United Nations Environment Programme, 2021).

REAL-LIFE EXAMPLE: STARTING A SCHOOL COMPOSTING PROGRAM

Jack, a high school senior, shares his experience starting a composting program at his school to reduce food waste and support sustainability:

"When I learned about the environmental impact of food waste, I knew I wanted to take action. I discovered that our school cafeteria was throwing away hundreds of pounds of food scraps every week, which ended up in landfills and contributed to greenhouse gas emissions.

I decided to start a composting program at my school. I researched different composting methods and reached out to local environmental organizations for guidance. I also recruited a team of student volunteers to help collect and process the food waste.

At first, it was a challenge to get everyone on board. Some students and staff were skeptical about the idea of composting, and we had to educate them about the benefits for the environment and the school. We held informational meetings, created posters and videos, and even hosted a "Compost Awareness Week" to raise awareness and encourage participation.

Over time, our composting program began to take off. We collected food scraps from the cafeteria and classrooms and used them to create nutrient-rich compost for our school garden. We also partnered with local farms and community gardens to donate excess compost.

Through this experience, I learned that small actions can add up to big impacts. By diverting food waste from landfills and creating healthy soil for plants, our composting program helped reduce greenhouse gas emissions and support local ecosystems. It also inspired other students and staff to adopt more sustainable habits in their own lives.

Now, as I graduate and move on to college, I plan to continue advocating for environmental responsibility and finding ways to make a positive impact. Whether it's starting a composting program, advocating for renewable energy, or simply making eco-friendly choices in my daily life, I know that every action counts in creating a more sustainable future."

INTERACTIVE ACTIVITY: CONDUCT A PERSONAL SUSTAINABILITY AUDIT

To identify areas where you can adopt more sustainable habits, try conducting a personal sustainability audit:

Energy use: Track your energy consumption for a week, including electricity, gas, and transportation. Identify ways to reduce your energy use, such as unplugging appliances, using LED light bulbs, or carpooling.

Water use: Monitor your water consumption for a week, including showers, laundry, and outdoor watering. Look for opportunities to save water, such as fixing leaky faucets, taking shorter showers, or using drought-tolerant landscaping.

Waste production: Keep a log of the waste you generate in a week, including food scraps, packaging, and single-use products. Consider ways to reduce your waste, such as composting, using reusable containers, or opting for products with minimal packaging.

Food choices: Track your food choices for a week, including the types of foods you eat and where they come from. Look for opportunities to make more sustainable choices, such as eating plant-based meals, buying local and organic produce, or reducing your food waste.

Purchasing habits: Keep a record of your purchases for a week, including clothing, electronics, and household items. Consider the environmental impact of your purchases, and look for ways to make more sustainable choices, such as buying secondhand, choosing eco-friendly products, or supporting companies with strong environmental practices.

Based on your audit, set realistic goals for adopting more sustainable habits in each area, and track your progress over time. Remember, small changes can add up to big impacts, and every action counts in promoting environmental responsibility.

ADVOCATING FOR CHANGE

In addition to adopting sustainable habits in your own life, you can also advocate for environmental responsibility on a larger scale. Here's why advocacy is so powerful:

- Collective action and advocacy can lead to systemic change, such as shifting policies, investments, and social norms toward sustainability.
- Raising awareness about environmental issues and solutions through education and outreach can mobilize more people to take action and demand change.
- Supporting eco-friendly businesses and products sends a market signal that sustainability is a priority and can give companies the incentive to adopt more responsible practices.
- Exercising your right to vote and engaging in the political

process ensures that environmental concerns are represented in decision-making at all levels of government.

- Volunteering and donating to environmental organizations amplifies their impact and supports critical work to protect and restore ecosystems, advance clean energy, and promote environmental justice.

Some ways to get involved and make a difference include:

Educate others: Share your knowledge about environmental issues and sustainable practices with friends, family, and community members to raise awareness and inspire action.

Join a club or organization: Participate in environmental clubs, organizations, or campaigns at your school or in your community to connect with like-minded individuals and work together for change.

Support eco-friendly businesses: Use your purchasing power to support companies and products that prioritize sustainability and environmental responsibility.

Vote and advocate: Use your voice and your vote to support political candidates and policies that prioritize environmental protection and sustainability.

Volunteer and donate: Give your time, skills, or resources to environmental organizations and initiatives that are working to protect the planet and promote sustainability (Kellogg, 2019).

By advocating for change and inspiring others to take action, you can help create support for environmental responsibility and sustainability and contribute to a healthier, more resilient world for all.

KEY TAKEAWAYS

- Understanding environmental issues like climate change, biodiversity loss, pollution, and resource depletion is the first step in promoting environmental responsibility.

- Adopting sustainable habits in your own life, such as reducing waste, conserving energy and water, eating sustainably, and traveling green, can have a significant positive impact on the environment.
- Youth engagement in environmental issues is critical for creating a more just and sustainable world for current and future generations.
- Conducting a personal sustainability audit can help identify areas where you can adopt more eco-friendly habits and set goals for change.
- Advocating for change through education, activism, support for eco-friendly businesses, voting, and volunteering can help create support for environmental responsibility and sustainability.

AFTERWORD

"The future belongs to those who believe in the beauty of their dreams" - Eleanor Roosevelt.

Congratulations on completing this comprehensive guide to essential life skills for teenage boys. Throughout this book, we have explored a wide range of topics and strategies to help you navigate the challenges and opportunities of adolescence and prepare for a successful and fulfilling future.

From developing financial literacy and digital citizenship skills to cultivating emotional intelligence, creativity, and cultural competence, the skills and knowledge you have gained will serve you well in all areas of your personal and professional life.

As you embark on the next chapter of your journey, remember that learning and growth are lifelong processes. Continue to seek out new experiences, challenges, and perspectives that will help you develop your skills, expand your horizons, and make a positive impact on the world around you.

Here are some key takeaways and action steps to keep in mind as you move forward:

1. **Financial literacy:** Create a budget, start saving and investing early, and learn about credit, debt, and taxes to build a strong financial foundation.

2. **Digital citizenship:** Protect your online safety and privacy, cultivate a positive digital footprint, and use technology in a responsible and ethical manner.

3. **Emotional intelligence:** Develop self-awareness, empathy, and healthy coping strategies to navigate relationships and challenges with resilience and compassion.

4. **Leadership and teamwork:** Seek out opportunities to practice and develop your leadership skills, and learn to collaborate effectively with others towards common goals.

5. **Cultural competence:** Educate yourself about different cultures and perspectives, engage in diverse experiences and conversations, and promote equity and inclusion in your communities.

6. **Health and wellness:** Prioritize self-care, healthy habits, and strong relationships to support your physical, mental, and emotional well-being.

7. **Goal-setting and decision-making:** Set SMART goals, gather information and support, and learn from both successes and failures to make informed and intentional choices about your future.

8. **Creativity and innovation:** Cultivate your creativity through diverse experiences, risk-taking, and collaboration, and use your skills to develop innovative solutions to challenges and opportunities.

9. **Conflict resolution and negotiation:** Practice active listening, expressing needs and interests, and finding win-win solutions to navigate conflicts and build stronger relationships.

10. **Continuous learning and growth:** Stay curious, open-minded, and proactive in seeking out new knowledge, skills, and experiences that will help you adapt and thrive in a changing world.

Remember, you have the power to shape your own future and make a positive difference in the world. By developing these essential life skills and applying them in your daily life and relationships, you can unlock your full potential and create a life of purpose, fulfillment, and impact.

So go forth with confidence, compassion, and courage, and know that you have the tools and support you need to succeed and thrive as a young man in today's world.

EMPOWER OTHERS WITH YOUR WORDS: LEAVE A LEGACY

"The two most important days in your life are the day you are born and the day you find out why." - Mark Twain.

Congratulations on completing "Life Skills for Teenage Boys"! You've taken a monumental step towards becoming the architect of your own future. The knowledge, insights, and strategies you've gained have undoubtedly equipped you with the tools to succeed in all areas of your life.

But your journey doesn't end here. In fact, it's just the beginning. Now, you have the opportunity to pay it forward and make a lasting impact on the lives of countless other teenage boys who are yearning for guidance, support, and inspiration.

By leaving a heartfelt review of this book on Amazon, you're not just sharing your thoughts—you're building a legacy of empowerment. Your words have the power to:

Illuminate the path to success for teenage boys who are feeling lost or overwhelmed.

Provide a sense of camaraderie and reassurance, reminding others that they're not alone in their struggles.

Inspire others to take action, embrace their potential, and create positive change in their lives.

To leave a review, simply click on this link or scan the QR code: https://www.amazon.com/review/review-your-purchases/?asin= B0D9ST7BHJ

Your review is more than just feedback; it's a gift of hope, encouragement, and guidance to teenage boys who are searching for answers. By sharing your story, you're not only validating the impact of this book but also creating a ripple effect of positive change that will touch lives for generations to come.

Thank you for being a force for good and for considering this opportunity to empower others with your words. Your voice matters, and your impact will be felt long after you close this book.

Go forth and conquer, knowing that you have the power to shape your future and inspire others to do the same.

With heartfelt gratitude,

A.E. Nicholls

P.S. - Your story is your superpower. Use it to uplift, empower, and transform the lives of teenage boys everywhere. Leave a review today and become the hero someone else has been waiting for.

FINAL THOUGHTS

"Success is not final, failure is not fatal: It is the courage to continue that counts" - Winston Churchill.

As we conclude this journey together, I want to leave you with a few final words of encouragement and advice:

Embrace your unique strengths and passions.

You have a special combination of talents, interests, and experiences that make you who you are. Don't be afraid to lean into your individuality and pursue paths that align with your authentic self.

Build strong, supportive relationships.

No one achieves success alone. Surround yourself with people who lift you up, challenge you to grow, and have your back through thick and thin. Be a good friend, family member, and community member in return.

Practice resilience and adaptability.

Life will inevitably throw curveballs and setbacks your way. Remember that every challenge is an opportunity to learn, grow, and develop new skills and perspectives. Cultivate a growth mindset, and don't be afraid to pivot or try new approaches when needed.

Find purpose and meaning in your pursuits.

While it's important to set goals and work hard, don't forget to also prioritize activities and causes that bring you joy, fulfillment, and a sense of connection to something bigger than yourself. Use your talents and passions to make a positive difference in the world.

Take care of yourself along the way.

Your physical, mental, and emotional well-being are the foundation upon which all your other successes are built. Make time for self-care, stress management, and healthy habits, and don't hesitate to seek help and support when needed.

As you embark on the next chapter of your life, know that you have a bright future ahead of you. The world needs your unique gifts, perspectives, and leadership now more than ever. Trust in your abilities, stay true to your values, and never stop learning and growing.

We believe in you and can't wait to see the incredible impact you will make. Here's to a lifetime of personal growth, meaningful connections, and positive change. The journey is just beginning, and we'll be cheering you on every step of the way.

BIBLIOGRAPHY

Adobe. (2016, April 27). Adobe study reveals generation gap in attitudes about creativity in the U.S. Retrieved from https://news.adobe.com/news/news-details/2016/Adobe-Study-Reveals-Generation-Gap-in-Attitudes-About-Creativity-in-the-US/default.aspx

American Heart Association. (2018). Added sugars. Retrieved from https://www.heart.org/en/healthy-living/healthy-eating/eat-smart/sugar/added-sugars

Anderson, M. (2018, September 27). A majority of teens have experienced some form of cyberbullying. Pew Research Center. https://www.pewresearch.org/internet/2018/09/27/a-majority-of-teens-have-experienced-some-form-of-cyberbullying/

AVID. (2021). What is the Cornell note-taking system? Retrieved from https://www.avid.org/what-is-the-cornell-note-taking-system

Baglioni, C., Spiegelhalder, K., Nissen, C., Voderholzer, U., & Riemann, D. (2016). Sleep and mental health. The Lancet Psychiatry, 3(2), 99-101. https://doi.org/10.1016/S2215-0366(15)00582-2

Barlett, C. P., DeWitt, C. C., Maronna, B., & Johnson, K. (2020). Social media use as a tool to facilitate or reduce cyberbullying perpetration: A review focusing on anonymous and nonanonymous social media platforms. Violence and Gender, 7(4), 147-152. https://doi.org/10.1089/vio.2020.0006

Bauman, S., & Baldasare, A. (2018). Cyber aggression among college students: Demographic differences, predictors of distress, and the role of the university. Journal of College Student Development, 59(1), 9-21. https://doi.org/10.1353/csd.2018.0001

Botting, L. (2019, September 12). How to create a budget: A step-by-step guide. Investopedia. Retrieved from https://www.investopedia.com/how-to-create-a-budget-5116603

Bowman, N. A. (2011). Promoting participation in a diverse democracy: A meta-analysis of college diversity experiences and civic engagement. Review of Educational Research, 81(1), 29-68. https://doi.org/10.3102/0034654310383047

Buffett, W. (2007). Quoted in multiple sources on the importance of self-investment.

CDC. (2021). Healthy eating for a healthy weight. Retrieved from https://www.cdc.gov/healthyweight/healthy_eating/index.html

Chekwa, E. (2018, June 4). 6 strategies for developing a leadership mindset in teenagers. Training Industry. Retrieved from https://trainingindustry.com/articles/leadership/6-strategies-for-developing-a-leadership-mindset-in-teenagers/

Churchill, W. (1941). Speech to the House of Commons, October 29, 1941. London: Hansard.

Connick, W. (2021, November 17). The importance of starting investing when you're young. The Balance. Retrieved from https://www.thebalance.com/why-start-investing-as-a-teen-4769571

Covey, S. (1989). The 7 Habits of Highly Effective People: Powerful Lessons in Personal Change. Free Press.

Doyle, A. (2021, April 15). Important teamwork skills that employers value. The Balance Careers. Retrieved from https://www.thebalancecareers.com/teamwork-skills-list-2063773

Doyle, A. (2022, February 2). Important leadership skills for workplace success. The Balance Careers. Retrieved from https://www.thebalancecareers.com/top-leadership-skills-2063782

Drucker, P. F. (1999). Management Challenges for the 21st Century. New York: Harper Business.

Dweck, C. S. (2006). Mindset: The new psychology of success. Random House.

Einstein, A. (n.d.). BrainyQuote.com. Retrieved from https://www.brainyquote.com/quotes/albert_einstein_133991

Emerson, R. W. (n.d.). BrainyQuote. Retrieved May 16, 2024, from https://www.brainyquote.com/quotes/ralph_waldo_emerson_386829

Experian. (2019, October 10). Why do I need credit? Retrieved from https://www.experian.com/blogs/ask-experian/why-do-i-need-credit/

Fernando, J. (2021, October 21). Good debt vs. bad debt: What's the difference? Investopedia. Retrieved from https://www.investopedia.com/articles/pf/12/good-debt-bad-debt.asp

Franklin, B. (1758). The Way to Wealth. Printed in Poor Richard's Almanack

Gates, B. (2024). 100 technology quotes to inspire & motivate. *DigitalDefynd*. Retrieved from https://digitaldefynd.com

Gates, B. (1995). The Road Ahead. Viking Penguin.

Gebel, M. (2020, March 27). 5 ways to spot fake news online, according to experts. Insider. Retrieved from https://www.insider.com/how-to-spot-fake-news-online-2020-3

Goleman, D. (1995). Emotional intelligence: Why it can matter more than IQ. Bantam Books.

Goleman, D. (2018). The emotionally intelligent leader. Harvard Business Review Press.

Gregoire, C. (2018, December 4). 18 things highly creative people do differently. The Huffington Post. Retrieved from https://www.huffpost.com/entry/creativity-habits_n_4808459

H&R Block. (2022). Taxes 101: Everything you need to know about filing taxes. Retrieved from https://www.hrblock.com/tax-center/irs/tax-responsibilities/taxes-101/

Harvard Law School. (2021, April 5). The negotiation skills you need for success. Harvard Law School Program on Negotiation. Retrieved from https://www.pon.harvard.edu/daily/negotiation-skills-daily/the-negotiation-skills-you-need-for-success/

Hofmann, S. G., Asnaani, A., Vonk, I. J., Sawyer, A. T., & Fang, A. (2012). The efficacy of cognitive behavioral therapy: A review of meta-analyses. Cognitive therapy and research, 36(5), 427-440. https://doi.org/10.1007/s10608-012-9476-1

Howlett, N., Pine, K., Orakçıoğlu, I., & Fletcher, B. (2013). The influence of clothing on first impressions: Rapid and positive responses to minor changes in male attire. Journal of Fashion Marketing and Management, 17(1), 38-48. https://doi.org/10.1108/13612021311305128

Hunt, V., Prince, S., Dixon-Fyle, S., & Yee, L. (2018, January). Delivering through diversity. McKinsey & Company. Retrieved from https://www.mckinsey.com/business-functions/people-and-organizational-performance/our-insights/delivering-through-diversity

Johnston, L. D., Miech, R. A., O'Malley, P. M., Bachman, J. G., Schulenberg, J. E., & Patrick, M. E. (2021). Monitoring the Future national survey results on drug use 1975-2020: Overview, key findings on adolescent drug use. Ann Arbor: Institute for Social Research, University of Michigan. Retrieved from https://www.drugabuse.gov/drug-topics/trends-statistics/monitoring-future

Kellogg, K. (2019, October 15). How to be an environmental advocate: 5 ways to make an impact. FoodPrint. Retrieved from https://foodprint.org/blog/how-to-be-an-environmental-advocate/

Khan Academy. (2021). About. https://www.khanacademy.org/about

Khoury, B., Sharma, M., Rush, S. E., & Fournier, C. (2015). Mindfulness-based stress reduction for healthy individuals: A meta-analysis. Journal of psychosomatic research, 78(6), 519-528. https://doi.org/10.1016/j.jpsychores.2015.03.009

Kilmann Diagnostics. (2021). An overview of the Thomas-Kilmann Conflict Mode Instrument (TKI). Retrieved from https://kilmanndiagnostics.com/overview-thomas-kilmann-conflict-mode-instrument-tki/

Kiva. (2021). About us. https://www.kiva.org/about

Leaper, D. (2019, April 19). How to find your personal style. GQ. Retrieved May 16, 2024, from https://www.gq.com/story/how-to-find-your-personal-style

Lieberman, C. (2019, March 18). Why you procrastinate (it has nothing to do with self-control). The New York Times. Retrieved from https://www.nytimes.com/2019/03/25/smarter-living/why-you-procrastinate-it-has-nothing-to-do-with-self-control.html

Love, K. (2018, March 6). Everyone is going through something. The Players' Tribune. https://www.theplayerstribune.com/articles/kevin-love-everyone-is-going-through-something

Mandela, N. (1994). Long walk to freedom: The autobiography of Nelson Mandela. Little, Brown, and Company.

Maxwell, J. C. (2002). Teamwork Makes the Dream Work. Thomas Nelson

Mayo Clinic. (2020). Water: How much should you drink every day? Retrieved from https://www.mayoclinic.org/healthy-lifestyle/nutrition-and-healthy-eating/in-depth/water/art-20044256

Mayo Clinic. (2021). Stress management. Retrieved from https://www.mayoclinic.org/healthy-lifestyle/stress-management/basics/stress-basics/hlv-20049495

McLaughlin, K. A., Koenen, K. C., Hill, E. D., Petukhova, M., Sampson, N. A., Zaslavsky, A. M., & Kessler, R. C. (2013). Trauma exposure and posttraumatic stress disorder in a national sample of adolescents. Journal of the American Academy of Child & Adolescent Psychiatry, 52(8), 815-830. https://doi.org/10.1016/j.jaac.2013. 05.011

Merikangas, K. R., He, J. P., Burstein, M., Swanson, S. A., Avenevoli, S., Cui, L., ... & Swendsen, J. (2010). Lifetime prevalence of mental disorders in US adolescents: results from the National Comorbidity Survey Replication--Adolescent Supplement (NCS-A). Journal of the American Academy of Child & Adolescent Psychiatry, 49(10), 980-989. https://doi.org/10.1016/j.jaac.2010.05.017

Misra, R., & McKean, M. (2000). College students' academic stress and its relation to their anxiety, time management, and leisure satisfaction. American journal of Health studies, 16(1), 41-51.

Mojtabai, R., Olfson, M., & Han, B. (2016). National trends in the prevalence and treatment of depression in adolescents and young adults. Pediatrics, 138(6). https://doi.org/10.1542/peds.2016-1878

Nagata, J. M., Cortez, C. A., Cattle, C. J., Ganson, K. T., Iyer, P., Bibbins-Domingo, K., & Baker, F. C. (2021). Screen time use among US adolescents during the COVID-19 pandemic: Findings from the Adolescent Brain Cognitive Development (ABCD) study. JAMA pediatrics, 176(1), 94-96. https://doi.org/10.1001/jamapediatrics.2021.4334

National Alliance on Mental Illness. (2022). Mental health by the numbers. Retrieved from https://www.nami.org/mhstats

National Bullying Prevention Center. (2022). What to do if your child is being bullied online. Retrieved from https://www.pacer.org/bullying/info/cyberbullying/what-to-do-if-your-child-is-being-bullied-online.asp

National Geographic Society. (2022, February 2). The world's biggest environmental issues. National Geographic Society. Retrieved from https://www.nationalgeographic.org/article/worlds-biggest-environmental-issues/

National Sleep Foundation. (2021). How much sleep do we really need? Retrieved from https://www.sleepfoundation.org/how-sleep-works/how-much-sleep-do-we-really-need

Nguyen, T. (2018). The history of the iPhone. ThoughtCo. https://www.thoughtco.com/who-invented-the-iphone-1992004

Nguyen, T. (2020, April 1). How technology is changing the way we communicate. The Washington Post. Retrieved from https://www.washingtonpost.com/technology/2020/04/01/technology-changing-communication/

Obama, B. (2009). Address at a Town Hall Meeting with Future Leaders of Europe. The American Presidency Project.

Obama, M. (2018). Becoming. Crown Publishing Group.

Oxford Learning. (2022, January 4). How to help your teenager get organized. Oxford Learning. Retrieved from https://www.oxfordlearning.com/help-your-teenager-get-organized/

Ozbay, F., Johnson, D. C., Dimoulas, E., Morgan, C. A., Charney, D., & Southwick, S. (2007). Social support and resilience to stress: from neurobiology to clinical practice. Psychiatry (Edgmont), 4(5), 35-40.

Pascarella, S. (2021, April 22). Best credit cards for students with no credit. Forbes.

Retrieved from https://www.forbes.com/advisor/credit-cards/best-student-credit-cards-no-credit/

Pew Research Center. (2021, April 7). Social media use in 2021. Retrieved from https://www.pewresearch.org/internet/2021/04/07/social-media-use-in-2021/

Pritchard, J. (2021, November 8). How teens can begin investing. The Balance. Retrieved from https://www.thebalance.com/a-guide-to-investing-for-teenagers-4174011

Quast, L. (2022, January 10). Maintaining a positive social media presence to help your career. Forbes. Retrieved from https://www.forbes.com/sites/lisaquast/2022/01/10/maintaining-a-positive-social-media-presence-to-help-your-career/?sh=4e7211f12409

Reagan, R. (1982, December 8). Address before a joint session of the Congress on the program for economic recovery. *Ronald Reagan Presidential Library*. Retrieved from https://www.reaganlibrary.gov/research/speeches/120882b

Rohn, J. (2024). Take care of your body. It's the only place you have to live. *Brainy Quote*. Retrieved from https://www.brainyquote.com/quotes/jim_rohn_147499

Roosevelt, E. (1960). You Learn by Living: Eleven Keys for a More Fulfilling Life. New York: Harper & Brothers.

Rosenberg, E. (2020, November 20). The 5 best automatic savings apps of 2022. The Balance. Retrieved from https://www.thebalance.com/best-automatic-savings-apps-4159705

Royal, J. (2021, August 18). What is a Roth IRA? Forbes. Retrieved from https://www.forbes.com/advisor/retirement/what-is-a-roth-ira/

Sundararajan, A. (2016). The sharing economy: The end of employment and the rise of crowd-based capitalism. MIT Press.

Scott, E. (2022, January 27). Using time management for stress relief. Verywell Mind. Retrieved from https://www.verywellmind.com/time-management-tips-for-stress-relief-3145186

Segal, J., & Smith, M. (2020, October). Conflict resolution skills. HelpGuide. Retrieved from https://www.helpguide.org/articles/relationships-communication/conflict-resolution-skills.htm

Sharma, A., Madaan, V., & Petty, F. D. (2006). Exercise for mental health. Primary care companion to the Journal of clinical psychiatry, 8(2), 106. https://doi.org/10.4088/pcc.v08n0208a

Shore, L. M., Cleveland, J. N., & Sanchez, D. (2018). Inclusive workplaces: A review and model. Human Resource Management Review, 28(2), 176-189. https://doi.org/10.1016/j.hrmr.2017.07.003

Shultz, D. (2021, July 1). Tips to help teens balance social media with the real world. National Geographic. Retrieved from https://www.nationalgeographic.com/family/article/tips-to-help-teens-balance-social-media-with-the-real-world

Steele, J. (2021, September 17). What is media literacy and why does it matter? Common Sense Media. Retrieved from https://www.commonsensemedia.org/articles/what-is-media-literacy-and-why-does-it-matter

Swart, J. (2022, March 25). 10 types of investments for beginners and tips to get

started. MagnifyMoney. Retrieved from https://www.magnifymoney.com/blog/
investing/types-of-investments/

Swan, R. (2009). Antarctica 2041: My Quest to Save the Earth's Last Wilderness.
New York, NY: Broadway Books.

Sweeting, H., Walker, L., MacLean, A., Patterson, C., Räisänen, U., & Hunt, K. (2015).
Prevalence of eating disorders in males: a review of rates reported in academic
research and UK mass media. International journal of men's health, 14(2). https://
doi.org/10.3149/jmh.1402.86

Tan, S. Y., & Tatsumura, Y. (2015). Alexander Fleming (1881–1955): Discoverer of
penicillin. Singapore Medical Journal, 56(7), 366–367. https://doi.org/10.11622/
smedj.2015105

TurboTax. (2021). Your guide to filing taxes as a freelancer. Retrieved from https://
turbotax.intuit.com/tax-tips/self-employment-taxes/your-guide-to-filing-taxes-as-
a-freelancer/L6ACNfKVW

Twain, M. (1897). Following the Equator: A journey around the world. American
Publishing Company.

United Nations Environment Programme. (2021, May 31). 10 ways to be more
sustainable. World Environment Day. Retrieved from https://www.worldenviron
mentday.global/get-involved/10-ways-be-more-sustainable

Walker, M. (2017). Why we sleep: Unlocking the power of sleep and dreams. Simon
and Schuster.

Wells, A. S., Fox, L., & Cordova-Cobo, D. (2016). How racially diverse schools and
classrooms can benefit all students. The Education Digest, 82(1), 17-24.

World Economic Forum. (2020, October). The future of jobs report 2020. World
Economic Forum. Retrieved from https://www3.weforum.org/docs/WEF_Fu
ture_of_Jobs_2020.pdf

ALSO BY A.E NICHOLLS

EXECUTIVE FUNCTIONING WORKBOOK FOR KIDS AGES 4 – 8

EXECUTIVE FUNCTIONING WORKBOOK FOR KIDS AGES 7 – 11

EXECUTIVE FUNCTIONING WORKBOOK FOR TEENS, AGES 13 - 18

Made in the USA
Coppell, TX
29 December 2024

43711836R00095